MW01077799

WHY
THE BAAL SHEM TOV
LAUGHED

WHY
THE BAAL SHEM TOV
LAUGHED

Fifty-two Stories about
Our Great Chasidic Rabbis

Sterna Citron

JASON ARONSON INC.
Northvale, New Jersey
London

This book was set in 12 pt. Schneidler by Lind Graphics of Upper Saddle River, New Jersey, and printed by Haddon Craftsmen in Scranton, Pennsylvania.

ISBN 0-87668-350-2

Library of Congress Number 92-39644

Manufactured in the United States of America. Jason Aronson Inc. offers books and cassettes. For information and catalog, write to Jason Aronson Inc., 230 Livingston Street, Northvale, New Jersey 07647.

Dedicated
to the precious memory
of my beloved father

Rabbi Eli Chaim Carlebach ז״ל

whose bedtime stories,
so warmly told to my sisters and me,
were chasidic tales
and whose lullabies,
so sweetly sung,
were chasidic *nigunim*

❉❉❉

Contents

CONTENTS

※※※※

Acknowledgments

My heartfelt thanks go to:

My friends who pushed, prodded, and encouraged me to write, among them Elizabeth Lund, Rivka Chroman, Liora Varon, Rochel Schochet, Shoshana Bracha Plotke, and others, and my sisters Sheina Berkowitz, Yocheved Baila (Billie) Dayan, Fraidy Laufer, and Esty Kugel, who, because of their high expectations of me, I could not let down,

Typists Yocheved Novack and Sherri Sakoff, Yocheved for her feedback and critiquing and Sherri for her punctiliousness and promptness,

Al Saunders of Newcastle Publishing, who has given me wise counsel at crucial times,

Enrique Gascon for generously giving his photographic expertise,

Publisher Arthur Kurzweil for realizing the possibility of expanding the one small story I gave him to an anthology of 52 stories, and to his able editors, especially Janet Warner,

My children, who, while always proud of their mother's achievements, were never afraid to tell the truth about anything she wrote,

My mother, Hadassa Carlebach, may she live many long years in good health, who has praised and encouraged my writing since I was a child,

And my husband, Rabbi Chaim Zev Citron, without whom this book could never have seen the light of day. He compiled the biographies on the *rebbes,* he helped me hunt for suitable stories, and he patiently advised me in the many decisions, big and small, that had to be made,

And finally, to the Lubavitcher *rebbe shlita,* who blessed me with "great and superlative success" in writing chasidic stories.

Author's Note

Two systems of dates are used in this book: the secular year is followed by the Jewish year in parentheses. The Jewish year is based on the traditional date of Creation.

REB YISROEL BAAL SHEM TOV

Born:	1698 (5450)
Died:	1760 (5520)
Lived in:	Medzhibozh (Podolia)
Best known as:	Founder of *Chasidus*

✳✳ 1 ✳✳

Why the Baal Shem Tov Laughed

ne Friday night the Baal Shem Tov suddenly laughed. He laughed once. He laughed twice. He laughed a third time.

No one knew why.

But that Friday night, in the town of Koznitz, many miles away, something wonderful happened.

It had started that Friday morning. Reb Shabsai, the book-binder, sadly said to his wife, "I did not make any money this week. We will not be able to buy anything for *Shabbos*. Not even candles. I am going to *shul* to say *tehillim* and learn."

He got dressed in his *Shabbos* clothes and left for *shul*. It was early, but what was there to do at home? There was no money to go shopping and no food in the house to cook. He would never ask anyone for anything either. Reb Shabsai hated asking people for things.

Reb Shabsai's wife sighed and looked around. "Well, at least I can clean up in honor of the *Shabbos*."

Saying that, she began dusting and polishing the furniture. She changed the beds and swept under them. She scrubbed and washed the floors.

Behind the furniture something seemed to sparkle. Reb Shabsai's wife bent down and picked up the sparkling objects and exclaimed, "What a surprise! Here is the jewelry I lost a long time ago. I will sell it and buy what we need for *Shabbos*."

The good woman rushed to the market. She sold the jewelry and with the money she bought the best of everything for *Shabbos*. There was even some money left over when she finished.

At home she cooked all the dishes quickly. At last she lit the *Shabbos* candles. The candles gleamed, the house shone, and the food smelled wonderful.

When Reb Shabsai came home from *shul* that Friday night, he did not look happy. From where had his wife gotten everything? Probably she had borrowed from the neighbors to pay for all of this. He wished she hadn't. But he wasn't going to argue about it on the holy *Shabbos*.

They ate the gefilte fish in silence. It was so tasty! Reb Shabsai couldn't help saying to his wife, "How I wish you hadn't gone to the neighbors!"

"But I didn't!" laughed his wife merrily. "You remember the silver jewelry I lost a long time ago? While I was cleaning the house for *Shabbos*, I found it. I got a nice amount of money for it and that's how I was able to buy all of this."

Reb Shabsai could hardly believe his ears! What a stroke of good fortune! How kind *Hashem* was to them! And to think he had suspected his wife of asking the neighbors for food! He jumped up and began to dance. His wife could not help dancing either. Together they joyfully sang and danced.

At that point, far away in Medzhibozh, the Baal Shem Tov laughed.

Next Reb Shabsai's wife served the chicken soup. It was even more delicious than usual. Again Reb Shabsai and his wife's hearts filled with happiness. They just had to dance! And so dance they did.

That was the second time the holy Baal Shem Tov laughed.

When Reb Shabsai's wife served the next generous course, they were overcome a third time with joy. What could they do but dance again? They danced and danced until they couldn't dance anymore.

That was the third time the Baal Shem Tov laughed.

A year later *Hashem* blessed them with their first child. He grew up to become the tzadik Reb Yisroel of Koznitz.

✳✳ 2 ✳✳

Dreams and Determination

Part 1

Little Moshe Yosef was an orphan from both father and mother by the age of 5. After that, his uncle brought him up.

Moshe Yosef was sent to *cheder* to learn how to read. But Moshe Yosef could not understand what his rebbe wanted from him. Try as hard as he could, he just could not master the *alef-beis*. The other boys in the *cheder* poked fun at poor Moshe Yosef. "Ha, ha, you are a dummy! You don't even know *alef-beis*!" they teased. In his heart of hearts, Moshe Yosef cried, but what could he say to his classmates? What they said was true. He did not know the *alef-beis*.

One day the *rebbe* caught the *cheder* children mocking the little orphan boy. "What are you doing?" he asked, shocked.

The students were silent.

"Don't you know Moshe Yosef is an orphan? He doesn't have a father or a mother. You must be very kind to him. If you make him sad he will cry and God will get very angry."

After that the children stopped making fun of Moshe Yosef.

Time passed. Moshe Yosef's classmates were already starting to learn Talmud while Moshe Yosef was still struggling with the letters of the *alef-beis*.

But Moshe Yosef did not give up. Finally, after tireless efforts, Moshe Yosef managed to learn all of the alphabet.

However, he could not master anything more than that, though he tried very hard.

Eventually Moshe Yosef stopped going to school. He moved into the home of Reb Refoel, the tinsmith, and became his apprentice. Reb Refoel taught his new student the skills needed to do the work of a tinsmith.

The tinsmith realized that his apprentice was ignorant and unlettered in Torah. Patiently he taught Moshe Yosef the blessings over food. At last Moshe Yosef knew them all.

While he did his tinsmithing, Reb Refoel would recite psalms or chapters from the *Mishnah* by heart. Moshe Yosef listened to him enviously. He wished he knew the psalms or *Mishnah* so that he could recite them while he worked. All he knew were the blessings over food. So Moshe Yosef recited those blessings over and over as he worked.

One day Reb Refoel heard his student saying the blessings over and over. "Moshe Yosef, it's not right to say God's name in vain. You must not say a blessing unless you are going to eat," he explained.

Moshe Yosef was crestfallen. But then he brightened up. Why, he knew the *alef-beis* too! He could say that! From then on, all day long he would recite the *alef-beis* by heart. He started from *alef* and went through the alphabet till *tuf.* Then he would say all the vowels. Then he would start again from the beginning.

Moshe Yosef lived in the home of the God-fearing tinsmith for several years. By now he knew all there was about being a tinsmith. His teacher said to him, "It's time you set up your own tinsmith shop. You will do very well on your own."

So Moshe Yosef took Reb Refoel's advice and opened up his own business. He was a competent tinsmith, he was honest, and he worked hard. The customers who came to him were pleased with his work and came back again and again. They told their friends about him and they too patronized his shop.

Soon the tinsmith business thrived. Moshe Yosef was delighted that now he was able to fulfill the *mitzvah* of helping the poor and the needy. He fulfilled this *mitzvah* very generously.

There was only one thing that marred Moshe Yosef's happiness. "I am still ignorant and unlearned," he sighed to himself frequently. "How I wish I could study Torah!"

When he reached marriageable age, Moshe Yosef married a girl named Fruma, who lived in a nearby village. They moved to Fruma's village, where Moshe Yosef opened up a new business. He succeeded to an even greater degree this time and became quite wealthy.

There was a Torah scholar in the village with whom Moshe Yosef became friendly. "You know," Moshe Yosef confided to his friend once, "I have a secret dream. I would like to become a Torah scholar like you."

"So why don't you study? If you study every day, you will become knowledgeable," the scholar replied.

Moshe Yosef shook his head resignedly. "I don't have a head for it. I went to *cheder* and I tried to learn for several years, but I could not."

"Well then, why don't you give charity to Torah scholars? Your money will enable them to study. What a wonderful privilege that will be! You will be like Zevulun, whose merchant ships paid for the Torah studies of his partner and brother Yissachar."

Moshe Yosef followed the scholar's advice. From that time on he secretly provided for Torah scholars so that they could continue studying. No one else knew about it. Moshe Yosef found some comfort in this, but he wasn't totally satisfied. His old dream still burned within him.

Part 2

Because the town where Moshe Yosef lived was very far from any big city, visitors rarely passed through. If anybody did happen to come by, the community council would throw lots to see who would be the lucky one to get the visitor.

One time a visitor came to the village, and the lot fell on Moshe Yosef and Fruma, who were overjoyed at the *mitzvah* of having a guest in their home.

The guest was an unusual person. He was a Torah scholar with a terrible skin disease. This did not upset Moshe Yosef and Fruma. Quite the contrary! They fed him nourishing foods, bathed him, and rubbed soothing ointment on his sores.

After a few days the guest said to his kind hosts, "Thanks to your attentive cares, I am feeling much better than I have felt in a long time. I think I'll be on my way."

"Oh, please stay with us a little longer," Moshe Yosef and Fruma begged. "It is such a rare treat for us to have a guest!"

"Well, if you insist," the visitor agreed.

"There's just one thing I am curious about," Moshe Yosef said. "How did you get those sores?"

"As you have been so good to me, I'll tell you," responded the scholar. "As a Torah student I desired to reach a higher level of understanding in my studies, so I fasted. Many days went by when I did not eat or drink. My health was affected and I got a bad skin disease."

The scholar's words struck deep into the heart of Moshe Yosef. It awoke his old dream of being a Torah scholar. "I too am willing to fast and to suffer in order to be learned," said Moshe Yosef determinedly to himself.

Moshe Yosef began fasting. Like the visiting scholar, he did not take food or drink into his mouth for many days. He prayed fervently to God. "Help me to understand Your holy Torah!" he implored.

Often he would take walks in the nearby woods. There he would recite psalms and feel very close to God.

One day while Moshe Yosef was in the woods he was overcome with a particularly strong longing to understand the Torah. Tears flowed freely from his eyes.

Suddenly he beheld the blurry image of a person through his tears. A Jew was wandering down the path in the woods and coming closer and closer. On his back he wore a knapsack, and in his hand he carried a walking stick.

The wanderer stopped when he reached Moshe Yosef. "Why are you crying, young man?" he asked softly.

Something about the wanderer made Moshe Yosef trust him. "I am crying because I cannot study Torah. I have fasted, I have prayed, I have said *tehillim*, and yet I am still an ignoramus."

The stranger gazed compassionately upon Moshe Yosef. "It isn't necessary to suffer and fast to become a Torah scholar. There is an easier way."

"There is?" Moshe Yosef asked unbelievingly.

"Give me all your money and worldly goods for charity, and then come travel with me for three years. I guarantee you that at the end of that time you will be a Torah scholar."

Moshe Yosef stood up. "I'm ready. Can we leave right now?"

The holy man laughed. "Go home and discuss it first with your wife. If she agrees, come back and meet me here in eight days."

Moshe Yosef anxiously presented his wife with the plan. To his relief she replied, "Isn't this what you longed for all your life? You have my support in this. I am ready to give up our wealth for you to carry out your dream of studying Torah. But only on one condition," she added. "I want the holy man to have one meal with us before you go off with him. Let us do the *mitzvah* of *hachnosas orchim* once before your trip."

Moshe Yosef thought it might be wise to discuss his plan with his father-in-law as well. His father-in-law was not happy about the idea at all. "How can you just leave your wife and children? Don't you have a responsibility to them? Besides, you support Torah scholars and you won't be able to do that anymore."

Moshe Yosef's head whirled. His father-in-law was right. He did have a responsibility to his family. He went back and forth in his mind. Yes go, no go. He couldn't decide.

The eighth day arrived and he still hadn't made up his mind. He shared his doubts with his wife.

"If you have all these doubts, you must not truly want to study Torah," Fruma answered spiritedly.

Moshe Yosef was taken aback by his wife's vehemence.

Fruma continued, "If you really, truly, desired it, you wouldn't hesitate for one moment. Don't worry about me and the children. We'll manage fine!"

His wife's fiery words filled Moshe Yosef with new energy.

As he hurried out to meet the *tzadik*, Fruma called out after him, "Don't forget my condition – please make sure he comes home with you."

When Moshe Yosef arrived at the designated spot in the woods, the wandering *tzadik* was there waiting for him. "Are you coming?" he inquired.

"Yes, I am," replied Moshe Yosef. "But my wife made one condition. I must bring you to my home to have supper with us. She loves having guests and she would not pass up this opportunity."

The *tzadik* said, "I accept her gracious invitation."

When the two men entered the house, they immediately noticed how festive the room looked. Tall white candles stood on the table and shed a warm glow over the room. The table was laden with all sorts of tasty-looking dishes.

"You have obviously gone to great lengths in preparing this meal," the amazed *tzadik* said to his hostess. "What is the reason for this feast?"

"It's a double celebration," she responded.

"Why double?" asked the visitor curiously.

"First," explained the righteous woman, "because we have the rare honor of having a guest at our table, and especially a saintly guest. And second, sometimes people lose their wealth and get nothing in return for it. But we are giving up ours so that my husband can go off to study God's holy Torah!"

The saintly man smiled at her explanation. The wonderful repast over, Moshe Yosef gave the *tzadik* the deed to all his money and property.

The *tzadik* turned to Fruma and said, "While your husband is gone, you may stay in the house and use the garden as well as the fruits and vegetables growing there." He also gave her a sack of flour and a sack of potatoes.

Fruma thanked him sincerely.

The next morning Moshe Yosef bid his family an emotional good-bye. Then he and the *tzadik* took off.

For three years, Moshe Yosef accompanied the holy man on his travels. During this time he immersed himself in the study of Torah and became a true scholar. He became proficient in the Talmud. The secrets of the Torah were revealed to him. His righteousness, too, was extraordinary, though he did his best to hide it.

After the three years, Moshe Yosef returned to his wife and children, but he was a different man—a hidden *tzadik*. The family moved to another town where no one knew them and where no one could find out how saintly Reb Moshe Yosef really was.

Years passed and Moshe Yosef and Fruma became old. When the time came, they passed away and their souls went up to heaven. Moshe Yosef was given a seat among the righteous *tzadikim* in the next world, and Fruma was given a place among the righteous women.

Every year when Moshe Yosef was elevated to a higher seat in the Garden of Eden (as is customary with *tzadikim* on their *Yahrzeit*), Fruma was also elevated, for Moshe Yosef's greatness was, after all, largely due to the self-sacrifice and determination of his wife.

And who was the holy wanderer? Why, it was the Baal Shem Tov, of course, who wandered through the back roads of the Ukraine before he was revealed to the world.

※ **3** ※

You Don't Get Something for Nothing

One of the most exalted *mitzvos* of the Torah is *hachnosas orchim* — hospitality to guests.

The Baal Shem Tov heard that the Jews of Sforad excelled in this *mitzvah* of *hachnosas orchim*. Curious to see if this reputation was truly deserved or not, he journeyed a great distance from Medzhibozh. He reached the town on *erev* Sukkos.

As his carriage rolled slowly through a little village, a Jew named Rachamim came out of his oil shop and called to him. "You are obviously from a distant land. Please do me the kindness of spending the *yom tov* with me. We have plenty of wine, fish, and meat for the holiday."

"I am touched by your generous offer, especially since I am a stranger to you," replied the holy man. "However, I must refuse. It is *yom tov* tonight and I must go to the town where I will have a *shul*, a *mikvah*, and an *esrog*."

"Ah," persisted Rachamim. "We have all those things here in the village." We have a *shul* with a *sefer* Torah, and we have a *mikvah* and an *esrog*. Please do me the honor of staying with me and my family. If you like, you can always walk to the town at any time, as it is within the *techum Shabbos*.

So the Baal Shem Tov consented to stay with Rachamin.

That night at the *yom tov* meal, the Baal Shem Tov noticed what a royal feast Rachamim and his family had prepared—

truly a table fit for kings and queens. The food was served attractively on dishes of fine china, crystal, and sterling silver. And what a large variety of tempting foods there were! Drinks, too, were plentiful. The oil merchant and his wife had spared no expense in honoring their guest and the holiday. So far the reports that the Baal Shem Tov had heard about Sephardic hospitality were coming true.

The next morning, which was the first day of the *yom tov*, the Baal Shem Tov walked to the town and *davened* there. Several people in the *shul* recognized the Baal Shem Tov. Soon the word spread that a holy mystic was in town. After the *davening*, one of the wealthy members of the community invited the Baal Shem Tov to his house, and the Baal Shem Tov accepted the invitation. The rich man invited everyone in the town to his *sukkah* and served them food and drink as they listened to teachings of the saintly mystic. The Baal Shem Tov could not help but marvel at the hospitality of the Sephardic Jews.

The people of the town jealously guarded over their guest and would not hear of his returning to the village until after *yom tov*.

After the *yom tov*, the Baal Shem Tov finally returned to the village. Rachamim greeted him warmly and begged him to stay. Rachamim was the perfect host. He attended to his guest's every need.

The Jews of the village and of the nearby town came again to Rachamim's home to hear the teachings of this unique man, and Rachamim welcomed them all in. He served them refreshments and drinks. They sat there well into the night, and Rachamim made sure all the while that everyone was comfortable and well cared for.

When it came time for the Baal Shem Tov to leave, he

asked his host, "I would like to bless you. With what shall I bless you?"

"Riches I have, thank God, and children, too," replied Rachamim. "What I would like is a guaranteed place in the world to come."

"Not so easy, my friend, not so easy," sighed the Baal Shem Tov. "For that you must first come to Medzhibozh, but Medzhibozh is a long, long way from here. You will have to travel through many countries. And the trip will be a costly one.

"I suggest you do the following," continued the great man. "Take with you a large shipment of fine wine, which is very scarce in Medzhibohz. Then you can sell it and earn yourself a handsome profit."

With that the Baal Shem Tov bade Rachamim farewell.

The oil merchant lost no time in carrying out the advice of the *rebbe*. He purchased hundreds of casks of fine wine and hired wagons and drivers to transport them to Medzhibozh. He spent his entire fortune in this venture.

Everything went smoothly during the first part of their travels. Rachamim and his wagons and drivers journeyed many days and many nights, from one city to another, through towns and villages, through forests and fields. They passed through one country after another.

One evening, Rachamim and his wagons were suddenly caught in a fierce downpour. They sought the nearest inn, where Rachamim ran to the innkeeper and asked, "Do you have a place where my wagon drivers can unload their cargo and keep it dry until the rain stops?"

"Just a little farther down the road, you will find some empty stores where you can unload your wagons. The drivers too can stay there overnight and guard your wares."

Rachamim led the wagons to the empty stores. He helped the drivers to stow all the wine in the dry, empty rooms. When he had made certain that everyone was comfortable and everything secure, he returned to the inn, where he spent the night.

After the morning prayers, Rachamim set off to the place where he had left the casks of wine the night before. To his shock, the stores were empty. There was nothing there: no wine, no wagons, no drivers.

Rachamim turned to go back to the inn. "I'll ask the inn-keeper if he knows where my wine and wagons are," he thought. He ran and ran but he couldn't find the inn. The inn wasn't where he thought it was.

"Where is the inn that was here?" he called out desperately to a woman passing by.

The passerby shrugged her shoulders. "You must be mistaken. There is no inn around here."

Down the street he saw a knot of men talking. He rushed over to them. "Do you know where the inn is?" he pleaded.

"What inn? We don't know of any inn around here." They looked at him as if he were crazy.

Rachamim continued to run, searching frantically, but he could find no inn, nor anyone who knew of one. The wine, wagons, and drivers had disappeared. Finally he gave up, exhausted.

"What should I do?" thought Rachamim. He had invested all of his money in the wine and wagons. Now he was penniless and far away from home, family, and friends.

Rachamim joined a group of Jewish wanderers who made their living by begging. He did not complain, not to the beggars, not to himself. If God wished him to be poor, what was there to complain about? He didn't whine about his fate and cry, "What did I do to deserve this?" He accepted his fate as God's will.

Rachamim and the wandering beggars roamed from one place to another. Months went by. One day they arrived in Medzhibozh, where the Baal Shem Tov lived.

The Baal Shem Tov, with his eyes of flesh that saw what was not seeable to others, said to his *shammes*, "A group of traveling paupers has just arrived in town. See if you can locate them. I would like them to spend *Shabbos* here with me."

The *shammes* hurried to comply with his master's request. He found the paupers and brought them to the Baal Shem Tov's home.

Friday night after *davening*, everyone gathered around the *Shabbos* table of the Baal Shem Tov. Disciples, guests, paupers—all were there to bask in the holy *Shabbos* atmosphere with the holy Baal Shem Tov. Everyone was surprised when the Baal Shem Tov singled out one of the paupers to sit next to him in the place of honor.

Rachamim (for it was the same Rachamim, though much changed) took the seat next to the *rebbe*. What does this mean, wondered the Baal Shem Tov's students silently. What had this poor mendicant done to deserve such a mark of respect?

"Do you remember what you asked me when I saw you on Sukkos?" queried the Baal Shem Tov.

Poor Rachamim had been through so much since then. What had he asked the holy Baal Shem Tov? He tried to recollect but it seemed so long ago. Suddenly his mind cleared. "I remember," Rachamim nodded his head.

"You asked me for a share in the world to come. You thought all you needed was my blessing and you would get *olam habo*, but *olam habo* is a very great and wonderful reward. One has to suffer and go through hardship to gain a share in it.

Before we met, you had an easy life. Everything you needed you had. Now you have endured heartache and pain without complaining and being bitter. You have truly earned your share in the world to come."

Rachamim was so overwhelmed with emotion he could not speak.

The Baal Shem Tov had more good tidings for Rachamim. "Your wagons and wine will turn up this Sunday."

The Baal Shem Tov explained to his *talmidim*, who were bursting with curiosity. "Rachamim and the people of his country practice the *mitzvah* of *hachnosas orchim* in a way that surpasses anything I have ever experienced in any of my travels. But that is not enough to merit the world-to-come. Rachamim still had to go through hardship. Now he is truly worthy of *olam habo*."

That Sunday, as the Baal Shem Tov had predicted, the wagons, with the wine in them, reappeared just as mysteriously as they had disappeared.

❋ 4 ❋

You Are Moshke and I Am Ivan

The wealthy Reb Mottel was one of the devoted disciples of the saintly Baal Shem Tov. He and his wife had only one child—Moshe. Wanting the very best for their child, they asked the Baal Shem Tov to take him into his home in Medzhibozh and train him for three years. That way Moshe'le ("little Moshe") could learn from the holy man how to be a God-fearing *chasidishe* Jew.

"Please take care of him," they asked. "And if you go anywhere, please make sure to take him with you."

The Baal Shem Tov agreed to their request. He took Moshe'le into his home, tended to him like a father and teacher, and helped him develop a good character.

In the three years that Moshe'le was there, the Baal Shem Tov did not go anywhere. He and Moshe'le stayed home.

The three years were almost up. It was the last *Shabbos* that Moshe'le would be there. The next morning his parents would come to pick him up.

Shabbos was over. The Baal Shem Tov said, "Hitch up the wagon. We are going for a ride."

Moshe'le was excited. He was finally going somewhere with his beloved mentor.

Moshe'le climbed into the wagon with the Baal Shem Tov and his disciples. The horses took off like the wind. They ran faster and faster till houses, trees, and fields looked like a blur. In a short time they had traveled a great distance. Moshe'le had experienced *kefitzas haderech*.

They arrived at an inn. It was far from Medzhibozh. No one there had ever heard of the saintly Baal Shem Tov and his disciples.

The Baal Shem Tov requested a private room, where he locked himself up. What mystical holy thoughts he was engrossed in, no one can say.

Why had he brought them there? Neither Moshe'le nor the disciples had any idea. Meanwhile, Moshe'le, slightly bored, began to hum a tune. He had a good voice and enjoyed singing. He sang a little louder.

Among the other guests at the inn was a rough-looking Ukrainian peasant. He liked the melodious sound of Moshe's singing. "Hey fella, what's your name?" he asked.

"My name is Moshke," answered the boy, giving the Russian version of his name.

The peasant called out to the innkeeper, "I like how this Moshke here sings. As long as he sings, I'll pay for everyone here to have whiskey."

"Moshke, keep singing!" the innkeeper urged Moshe, excited at the prospect of making a large amount of money. "I'll pay you for it."

But Moshe had been taught always to ask his teacher for permission. "If the Baal Shem Tov says I may, then I will," he replied.

The innkeeper hurried to the Baal Shem Tov's room. He opened the door and asked, "Do you allow your boy to sing for my customers?"

The holy man replied, "Yes, he has my permission."

With that, the peasant swung Moshke up in his great big arms on to the table. "Now sing," ordered the Ukrainian.

The young boy stood on top of the table and sweetly sang a *nigun*. Pushing back the table and chairs, the Ukrainian began to dance. He kicked up his heels and jumped high in the air. He punctuated his dance with cries of *"Ti Moshke a ya Ivan!"* ("You are Moshke and I am Ivan!")

"Pass around the drinks!" Ivan ordered the innkeeper. The innkeeper gladly did as he was told. "Bottoms up," cried Ivan, as he gulped down one shot of whiskey after another.

Eventually, Ivan was too exhausted to dance anymore. Moshke got down from the table.

Just then the Baal Shem Tov emerged from his room. Everyone climbed back into the wagon and returned home.

The next morning, Moshe's parents came and took him home.

Several years passed. Moshe was older now, and he had gotten married. The night he sang in the inn was completely forgotten.

Moshe had to travel for his business. Traveling in the time of the Baal Shem Tov was fraught with much more danger than it is now. Highway robbers roamed the countryside.

One of Moshe's business trips took him through a wild and lonely stretch of woods. Suddenly a band of robbers attacked him. They seized all his possessions. They were going to kill him. "Please, spare me! Don't kill me!" pleaded Moshe. "What good does it do you? You already took everything of mine!"

The robbers could not decide what to do with him. "Okay, okay, be quiet a minute. We'll take you to our chief. He'll decide what to do with you. Maybe he'll be in a good mood."

They hustled him off to their chief.

"Chief, we wanted to kill this man, but he whined so much that we figured you'd know better what to do with him." They waited to hear the chief's decision.

The chief looked the prisoner in the face and gave a start. "What's your name?"

"My name is Moshke," answered Moshe.

"Don't you know me?" asked the chief.

Moshe gazed at the rough features and muscular build of the man in front of him. "No, I don't."

"I remember you, though. You were much younger then. You came to the inn in these woods once – you and a rabbi and a bunch of other people – and you sang for me."

Memories crowded into Moshe's head. "I remember now. You are Ivan. You danced and shouted, *'Ti Moshke a ya Ivan!'*"

21

Ivan looked pleased. "That's right. We had a good time that night."

Then Ivan became serious. "Lucky for you my men didn't kill you on the spot. But from now on, I'll make sure you don't get hurt.

"Men!" yelled Ivan. "Moshke is an old friend of mine. I don't want him hurt. Give him back everything you took from him. Escort him safely out of the woods. If one hair on his head gets messed up, you'll have to answer for it!"

So the band of highwaymen returned Moshe's money and all his things and accompanied him out of the woods. From there Moshe made his way back home safely.

The Baal Shem Tov had foreseen all this years before, which was why he had brought Moshe to the inn to sing before Ivan. And that foresight on the part of the Baal Shem Tov saved Moshe's life.

✳ 5 ✳

Miracle in Constantinople

Part 1

A few days before Pesach, the Baal Shem Tov's daughter crouched by a small stream in the city of Constantinople as she washed her father's shirt for the holidays.

What, you may well ask, were the Baal Shem Tov and his daughter doing in Constantinople, so many hundreds of miles away from his town in Medzhibozh in the Ukraine?

The Baal Shem Tov was in Constantinople because he wanted to go to Israel. Having always yearned to go up to the holy land, he had finally resolved to make the trip. Heaven, however, had other plans for him. The Baal Shem Tov was not destined to live in Israel. On the way there, he found himself stranded in the city of Constantinople, accompanied only by his devoted daughter Aidel.

Aidel was thinking sad thoughts as she scrubbed and washed. They were all out of money, and Pesach was fast approaching. How would they buy *matzoh*? And wine? From where would they get all that they needed for the holiday? Whom could they turn to in this strange city? They didn't know a soul!

Aidel became so depressed that she started to cry. Her tears dripped onto the laundry, mixing with the suds.

"Young lady!" a man's voice called to her. She looked up to see a Jewish man, obviously well-to-do, looking down at her sympathetically. "What's the matter?" he asked.

His tone was so kind that Aidel could not resist pouring out her heart to him. "I'm crying because Pesach is coming," she tearfully replied, "and we are out of money. We cannot buy food or *matzoh*. We don't know anyone here to turn to. My father is a wonderful man. All day long he sits in the *beis midrash* and learns. I would hate to see him suffer! And here Pesach is coming closer, and all I can do to prepare for the holiday is wash our clothes."

"Please do me the honor of spending Pesach in our home," responded the stranger, whose name was Meir. "I will write down my name and address. Please give it to your father and tell him that I extend a heartfelt invitation to both of you."

Meir was a wealthy and respected member of the Jewish community of Constantinople. He was happy to have an opportunity to do this very great *mitzvah*. It was actually many *mitzvos* in one, he realized—inviting guests, feeding the poor, and honoring a righteous scholar.

Aidel flew home on wings of air. As soon as her father returned home, she ran to him, crying, "Father, father, a kind Jewish man invited us to spend Pesach with him."

The Baal Shem Tov was thrilled. "Thanks be to *Hashem* for for His eternal kindness! He has not forsaken us after all!"

Erev Pesach in the morning, while the Baal Shem Tov was studying as usual in the *beis midrash*, Meir approached him and introduced himself. "Excuse me. I am Meir. Perhaps your daughter told you that I met her? My family and I would be greatly honored if you and your daughter joined us for the holiday."

The Baal Shem Tov replied, "I gratefully accept your invitation." Reb Meir, awestruck by the radiant countenance of the *tzadik* from Medzhibozh, waited respectfully until the Baal Shem Tov was finished studying. Then they went to pick up Aidel and from there proceeded to the wealthy man's mansion, which stood in the great marketplace.

Reb Meir served his guests the last *chometz* meal. Then he gave them honey cake and *branfen*. It felt good to finally have something solid in their stomachs.

"It is my custom," Reb Yisroel Baal Shem said to his host, "to take a nap until *Minchah* time so that I may be well rested for the *seder*. Is there a private room I can use?" Meir led the saintly man to a private room with a bed in it. Reb Yisroel lay down and went to sleep.

"*Minchah* time!" came the call. But Meir's guest did not wake up. Meir thought he would peek into his room and gently awaken him. He was stunned to behold the Baal Shem Tov, fast asleep, tears streaming down his face, crying in his sleep! Meir was amazed. Quietly he withdrew. He did not dare to disturb Reb Yisroel after what he had seen.

Soon the Baal Shem Tov woke up. "We are late for *Minchah!*" he shouted. He quickly washed his hands. "Let us hurry so that we can start the *seder* early," he said. He talked about things that Meir could not understand—about God, who performs miracles, reveals secrets, and unravels mysteries.

What was his distinguished guest talking about? Meir had no idea. Nor could he comprehend why his holy guest had cried so much while he slept. Meir dared not ask the saintly man anything. He just waited and wondered.

After they *davened Minchah*, the Baal Shem Tov spoke to Meir. "I have a beautiful story for you, but I will tell it to you after we read the *Haggadah* tonight."

They *davened Maariv*. Meir invited his guest to join him for the *seder* at the table. How the crystal and silver sparkled on the table! How festive and splendid everything looked! The Baal Shem Tov was so happy that his face shone with joy. Gazing upon him, Meir and his family were not sure whether they had a man or an angel for a guest.

Kiddush was said, and the first of the four cups of wine drunk. The *Haggadah* was recited. Then the second cup was drunk. Meir could not bear the suspense. He had to understand what had taken place that afternoon. His curiosity overcame his awe of the *tzadik*. "Perhaps now the *rebbe* could explain to us what happened today?" he wondered, using the third person out of respect.

The saintly man responded in a half-smile. "When we have finished reciting the *Haggadah*, I will explain everything."

They continued reciting the *Haggadah*. They ate the Passover meal and chanted the *Birkas HaMazon*. Now they were up to the part of the *Haggadah* called *Hallel*—Praise.

Here the *tzadik* paused. With great fervor, he proclaimed God's praises. "He performs great wonders," he exclaimed with all his heart and soul. "He reveals that which is concealed." He repeated these phrases over and over, to the astonishment of everyone at the *seder* table. But the Baal Shem Tov's countenance radiated such holiness that no one dared to interrupt him with questions.

The *Haggadah* over, the Baal Shem Tov was now ready to tell his story. Late as it was, everyone waited with bated breath to hear the explanation of the strange things they had seen and heard. Following is what the Baal Shem Tov said.

Part 2

In every generation there are enemies who rise up against our people. God saves us from their clutches. This is exactly what occurred in the story I am about to tell you.

Not very long ago, there ruled in Constantinople a very good sultan. A just and kind ruler, he especially liked the Jews. In fact, his chief adviser was Jewish. Every time the sultan had to make an important decision, he always first consulted with Moshe, his cherished adviser.

Among the ministers of the sultan's cabinet, Moshe had many enemies who envied him because of his exalted position and hated him simply because he was Jewish. But he knew they could do nothing to him because he was the sultan's favorite.

Years went by. The sultan died. His only son was sent for from Paris, where he had been studying political science and world history. He returned to Constantinople and became the new sultan.

Moshe's enemies thought that they could influence the new

sultan against Moshe. After all, the sultan was young and impressionable. Perhaps he would listen to their insinuations. So they whispered in the sultan's ears hints of Moshe's disloyalty. The new sultan, however, did not believe them. "If my father thought so highly of him," he reasoned, "surely he must be a very worthy and loyal adviser. I shall continue to consult with him on all important decisions, just as my father did."

But there was one minister who would not give up—Mustafa. Mustafa hated Jews in general and Moshe in particular. He abhorred them so deeply so that he could not eat or sleep normally. Life was meaningless so long as the Jews continued their peaceful existence.

It was *erev* Pesach. Moshe asked the sultan for permission to speak. He was granted permission.

"Your Highness," he said, in his most ingratiating voice, "you are a new sultan, and the people have not yet had a chance to see you. Your Highness should parade through the streets tonight on your royal white horse with your servants and noblemen behind you in their smartest uniforms. Then all the people will come out and greet you."

The sultan liked Mustafa's idea. That night the royal cavalcade went out. First royal musicians blew their trumpets announcing "His Most Exalted Highness Sovereign, Emperor of the Byzantine Empire." Then the sultan, dressed in his most resplendent garments, appeared astride a mighty white steed. There followed rows and rows of guards, soldiers, and bands, all in smart uniforms.

The streets of Constantinople were lined with crowds of people waiting to catch a glimpse of the new sultan. "Long live the sultan!" they shouted. Everywhere people were excited and happy. The sultan, too, was thrilled to see the multitudes of his loyal subjects.

Mustafa led the sultan to the Jewish quarter of Constantinople. The streets were empty. The sultan could see lights in the houses and people assembled round their tables singing and drinking. But no one had come out to greet him. "Where is everybody?" he asked, a little hurt.

"Oh, the Jewish people don't care about you," replied Mustafa carelessly. "They're all at home having a party. They couldn't be bothered to come out to greet their new sultan."

Of course this wasn't true and Mustafa knew it. The Jews were home, having their *seder*, since it was the first night of Pesach.

The king could not believe Mustafa at first. "Aren't they afraid that I'll get angry and punish them?" he asked.

"No, they're not afraid of Your Highness," answered the clever Mustafa smoothly. "They know that your adviser Moshe will protect them, since Your Highness listens to everything he says."

The king was outraged. "What shall I do about it?" he asked indignantly. "This cannot be allowed to go on!"

"Moshe must be killed and the Jewish people banished from Your Highness's empire," Mustafa responded firmly. "Your Highness need not be bothered with the details. If you give me the royal ring, I will take care of drawing up the decrees for Moshe and the Jews."

"I will do that," said the angry sultan. He removed the ring from his finger and handed it to Mustafa.

Mustafa hurried home to tell his family of his success. All of them were exuberant at the news. All night long they made plans. They prepared a decree that said, "All the Jews shall be henceforth expelled from all the countries under the Byzantine Empire, and the chief adviser, Moshe, shall be hanged for treason." Mustafa and his family erected gallows from which to hang the unsuspecting Moshe.

Back at the palace, the sultan told the royal family of his plan. His mother was shocked. "Don't you know what happens if you start up with the Jewish people? Look at Pharaoh! Look at Haman – and he didn't even *do* anything to them. He only planned to. I don't want anything like that happening to you! Besides," she added, "the Jewish people are good for the economy. Why, it would be foolish to expel them!"

"Well, it's too late now," replied the sultan gloomily. "I gave that sly fox Mustafa my royal ring. Once he seals the document with my ring, it's permanent."

"Let's ask Moshe for advice," his mother answered. "He's resourceful. Maybe he'll find a way out."

Messengers were dispatched to Moshe. When he opened the door and saw who was there, he nearly collapsed. Messengers from the sultan in the middle of the night usually meant only one thing – immediate execution.

With a pounding heart, Moshe presented himself before the sultan and his mother, bowing low before them. "I have come at the behest of the sultan," he said trembling.

"We must speak to you privately," the sultan and his mother told Moshe. They entered the sultan's private chamber. The sultan related to Moshe everything that had happened the day before with Mustafa.

"You must think of a way to get the ring back as fast as possible!" the sultan's mother urged. "If not, catastrophe will surely befall you and your people. There will be nothing the sultan can do to help you."

Moshe thought quickly. "I suggest you assemble the palace guards and tell them that while Your Highness was out riding tonight, your ring was stolen. Tell them you think that the person who stole it probably intends to kill you while you are still asleep in the early morning. Whoever comes to the gates and presents the ring should be seized and immediately hanged."

"Do you really think that will work?" the sultan asked doubtfully.

"I know Mustafa pretty well. He hates me so much he won't waste one minute. It won't take him long to get here."

Sure enough, Mustafa soon showed up at the palace gates, waving the royal ring disdainfully. "Come on, let's go, open up the gate for me. Don't you have any respect for the sultan's own ring?"

"Respect for a scoundrel like you? We have you now, you ring stealer, you would-be sultan's assassin!" And before Mustafa could say a word, the guards snatched the ring out of his grasp, seized him, and tied him up.

"This is a mistake. A terrible mistake! I didn't steal the ring. The sultan himself gave me the ring."

"Do you expect us to believe that? We knew you were coming. We were warned about you." They mocked him as they began erecting a scaffold to hang him.

"I'll prove to you that I'm telling the truth! The sultan himself gave me the ring so I could seal a decree banishing the Jews and hanging Moshe. If you don't believe me, I'll even show you the gallows I prepared for Moshe to dangle from."

"Show us!" the guards challenged him.

Mustafa led them to the gallows. "You see?" he pointed to them. "Now do you believe me?"

A guard suggested, "Why bother setting up our own scaffold? We have one ready right here!"

So the guards hanged Mustafa from the very gallows he had prepared for his enemy.

"Now, my friends," concluded the saintly Baal Shem Tov, "do you understand why I cried when I slept? God had revealed to me in my sleep the terrible tragedy awaiting the Jews of Constantinople. I entreated Him to save them. Praised be God, He accepted my pleas and the decree was annulled. That is why when I woke up I blessed God and thanked Him for disclosing the hidden decree to me and for accepting my prayers that the decree be anulled.

"If you have any doubt that the story I told you is true, you will see Moshe returning in the morning from the sultan's palace, and we'll ask him what happened."

The family went to sleep for a few hours. The next morning they awoke, washed their hands, and ran to look out the window. Sure enough, Moshe was soon seen coming from the direction of the palace.

"*Gut yontif*, Moshe," the Baal Shem Tov addressed him. "Doesn't God perform great miracles? You never dreamed such a terrible decree would fall upon you and the Jewish community, did you? But now, out of that calamity has come the salvation of the Jews – the evil Mustafa is dead!"

"Yes," agreed Moshe joyfully, "he'll never plot against us again."

"And you, Moshe, merited to be the one through whom God saved the Jewish people from banishment," the Baal Shem Tov pointed out.

Soon all the Jews of the town heard about the terrible punishment that had almost befallen them and how they were miraculously saved. That morning everyone gathered in *shul* to *daven* with special *kavanah* and sing the *Hallel* with unusual devotion.

Meir then invited all the people in the *shul* to come to his home to see his righteous guest and hear the teachings of the holy rabbi whose prayers had saved the Jewish people of Turkey from a terrible decree.

✳✳ 6 ✳✳

Reb Michel Becomes a *Baal Teshuvah*

Looking rather downcast, a Jew approached the *tzadik* Reb Yechiel Michel of Zlotshov. "I need your help, *Rebbe*," he said in a broken voice. "Last Friday night I violated the *Shabbos*. I feel so bad about it."

Reb Michel's eyes widened in shock. "How could you do such a thing?"

Shamefacedly Reb Yiddel, as he was called, replied in a barely audible whisper, "I was on my way home last Friday afternoon, when my wagon suddenly broke down. I managed to fix it and to drive home. But by the time I got there, it was nighttime. I had desecrated the *Shabbos!*"

"That is a serious transgression," Reb Michel shook his head. "Atoning for it will be difficult and painful. In the wintertime, you must lie outside in the cold snow and take baths in ice-cold water. This will arouse in you thoughts of true *teshuvah*."

Reb Yiddel thanked the *tzadik* and returned home. "How can a weak and frail person like me survive such a penance?"

he sighed. He tried his best to do as Reb Michel had instructed, but he did not have the stamina to continue with it.

"What shall I do now?" wondered Reb Yiddel sadly. In his heart he yearned to make up for his sin and be innocent of any transgression, but how could he wipe this sin off his record?

Just then, news reached Reb Yiddel that the Baal Shem Tov was visiting in the town of Chadirklov, close to Reb Yiddel's town of Broisilav. The Baal Shem Tov's saintliness and piety were known far and wide. "Perhaps the Baal Shem Tov will give me an easier atonement," Reb Yiddel said to himself. He became a little more hopeful at the thought.

Reb Yiddel climbed onto his wagon and drove to Chadirklov. There he told the Baal Shem Tov what had happened to him the Friday night before. "What can I do to atone for it?" he begged to know. He hoped the Baal Shem Tov's *Tikun* would be easier than Reb Michel's.

"Buy candles and bring them to the *beis midrash* this Friday," responded the holy mystic.

Reb Yiddel stood there as if paralyzed. Had he heard right? It was too easy. How could such a light *Tikun* atone for such a serious sin?

Noticing Reb Yiddel's confusion, the Baal Shem Tov asked, "Why do you act so surprised?"

"Because you gave me a much easier *Tikun* than Reb Michel did." Reb Yiddel told the Baal Shem Tov about Reb Michel's demanding atonement and how difficult it was for him to do.

"Do what I tell you, Reb Yiddel, and that will be enough," the Baal Shem Tov assured him.

That Friday, Reb Yiddel bought candles and took them to the *beis midrash*. The *shammes* of the *shul* was nowhere to be found, so Reb Yiddel set up the candles and lit them himself.

Suddenly a dog ran into the *beis midrash*, seized the candles in his jaws, and crushed them between his teeth!

Reb Yiddel's shoulders sagged in despair. "My *teshuvah* has obviously not been accepted by heaven," he concluded.

Once again, Reb Yiddel made his way to the Baal Shem Tov and informed him of what had occurred.

"It seems to me," said the holy man after some deliberation, "that Reb Michel is displeased with my interference. However, don't let that trouble you. Bring the candles again to the *beis midrash*. I promise you that it won't happen again." The righteous leader added, "I would also like you to give a message to Reb Michel from me. Please tell him that I would like him to be my guest this *Shabbos*."

Upon his return to Broisilav, Reb Yiddel stopped at Reb Michel's home and delivered the message. Reb Michel accepted the invitation.

That Friday, Reb Michel harnessed his wagon and climbed aboard. The Baal Shem Tov was staying at Chvostov, which was only a short distance away. He should arrive there in very little time, Reb Michel thought.

Things did not go as the *tzadik* had planned, however. He took one wrong turn and then another. The sun was already setting. *Shabbos* had begun and here he was – still in the forest! Reb Michel got out of his wagon and walked toward Chvostov. When he reached the town, it was already pitch dark. Totally distraught, he arrived at the lodgings of the Baal Shem Tov, where he found the holy *rav* standing, *becher* in hand, about to recite the *kiddush*.

"You feel pretty bad, don't you?" asked the Baal Shem Tov softly. "Now you know how Reb Yiddel felt when he desecrated the *Shabbos*. You never sinned before this," the Baal Shem Tov continued, "and so you never truly understood how bad a good person feels after sinning and even after repenting. It is not necessary to undergo harsh penances to repent. All that is needed is a truly broken heart."

The next Friday night, Reb Yiddel lit his candles. And this time they remained burning, true to the Baal Shem Tov's promise.

REB DOV BER OF MEZHIRECH

Born:	1704 (5462)
Died:	1772 (5533)
Lived in:	Mezhirech, Volhynia
His _rebbe_:	The Baal Shem Tov
Best known as:	The main disciple of the Baal Shem Tov and _rebbe_ of many outstanding disciples
Also called:	_Magid_ of Mezhirech

✳ 7 ✳

The *Tefillin* of the Great *Magid*

Part I

The following story is about a very special pair of *tefillin*—the *tefillin* of HaMagid HaGadol, the *Magid* of Mezhirech.

The story begins after the passing away of the holy Rizhiner *rebbe* Reb Yisroel, the great-grandson of the *Magid* of Mezhirech. The Rizhiner *rebbe*'s sons gathered to divide up their father's inheritance.

"Let's not quarrel about who gets what," said one of the brothers.

"That's right," they all agreed. "No fighting."

"I have an idea," one of the brothers announced. "Let's each make a list of what we would like to have and put our lists into sealed envelopes. Then one of us will read the lists aloud, and everyone will get what he asked for."

The brothers liked the idea. They wrote their lists and slipped them into envelopes, which they sealed.

Then someone came up with a better idea. "Why don't we throw lots instead? However the lot comes out, that's what we'll get. That way no one can complain. It will all be in God's hands."

"That's a better idea," agreed the brothers. No sooner said

than done. The brothers threw lots to see who would get which of their holy father's possessions.

With hearts pounding, everyone waited to see who would get what. Everyone was especially anxious to learn who would get the *tefillin* of their father, which had originally belonged to their great-great-grandfather, the holy *Magid* of Mezhirech, successor of the Baal Shem Tov.

The *tefillin* fell to the lot of Reb Dovid Moshe. The other brothers heaved a sigh of regret. As for Reb Dovid Moshe, he could barely hide his ecstasy.

"Let's look in the sealed envelopes just to see what each of us wrote," suggested the oldest brother, Reb Avrohom Yaakov, after the inheritance had all been divided.

Each was curious to see what the other brother had wanted. All the brothers had long lists, and each of them had included the *tefillin* on their list.

Reb Dovid Moshe's list was different. It wasn't really a list at all, for there was only one thing written on it: "the *tefillin* of my father." That's all he had wanted. His brothers gasped in amazement when they saw that. It was obviously God's hand that had made the *tefillin* fall into Reb Dovid Moshe's possession.

The brothers returned to their homes. Reb Dovid Moshe, too, returned to his home in Potek. Each morning he donned the *tefillin* before *davening*, and each morning he felt its holiness and was uplifted and transported by it.

The oldest brother, Reb Avrohom Yaakov, returned to Sadgora. Now and then he would think about his father's *tefillin* and breathe a sigh of regret. How he wished it had fallen to his share!

One night – it was on a Chanukah night – the Sadgorer *rebbe*, as he was called, poured out his heart to his *chasidim*.

"Jealousy is usually destructive and deadly," said the Sadgorer *rebbe*. "But sometimes there is good jealousy, such as the jealousy of Matisyahu and his five sons, the Maccabees. They were jealous for God and were ready to fight to the death to uphold God's name and the Torah.

"Then," he continued, "there is jealousy between scholars. That too is a good thing, for it leads to increased Torah study. Jealousy between righteous people leads to an increased awe of God.

His *chasidim* listened, mystified. What was their *rebbe* driving at? With the next sentence they knew.

"And I," concluded the Sadgorer *rebbe*, looking dreamily into the distance, "I envy my brother Reb Dovid Moshe, because he gets to put on the holy *tefillin* of my great-grandfather, the *Magid*, every single day."

Two impetuous, hotheaded lads were present that evening, who could not bear to see their *rebbe* unhappy. Why, if their beloved *rebbe* lacked something, they would get it for him! He needn't be unhappy any longer! They were ready to do anything for him!

Without telling anyone of their plans, they quietly left town, traveled to Potek, and located the *tefillin* of the great *Magid*. When no one was around, they secretly removed the *parshios* from inside the *tefillin* and replaced them with ordinary *parshios*. No one could tell by looking at the outside of the *tefillin* that anyone had tampered with them. Then the youths made their way back to Sadgora with the holy *parshios*.

At the first opportunity, they gave the *parshios* to the *rebbe*. "We knew how much you longed for these *tefillin*, so we got them for you."

The *rebbe* stared in disbelief at the *parshios* in front of him. He picked them up reverently and scrutinized them. There was no question about it. They were the *tefillin* of the *Magid.* He turned his darkened gaze upon the youths. "How did you get them?" Something about the way he asked made the lads tremble.

"W-w-w-we-e-e-e-exchanged the *parshios.* We thought you wanted them," they stammered.

"You mean you *stole* them?" the *rebbe's* voice was very stern. "Foolish youths! How could you have done such a thing?"

The boys hung their heads in shame. They had meant to do a good thing. They had wanted to make their *rebbe* happy. Instead they had incurred his wrath.

The Sadgorer *rebbe* wrapped the *parshios* up in a silk cloth. Then he addressed the people there. "None of you may repeat what you saw or heard here now. Prepare yourselves for a trip. We will be going to Potek to return the *tefillin* to my brother."

How the lads wished they could undo what they had done! They felt miserable.

Upon the arrival of the Sadgorer *rebbe* and his *chasidim* (the two young lads among them), Reb Dovid Moshe greeted them warmly. The brothers embraced. Reb Dovid Moshe attended to all the guests, making sure they ate well and had comfortable lodgings.

The next morning in *shul,* the Sadgorer *rebbe* watched out of the corner of his eye as his brother prepared to pray. He noticed his brother had two pairs of *tefillin* – an ordinary pair and the *Magid's* pair. Reb Dovid Moshe first picked up the *Magid's* *tefillin* and held it lovingly in his hands. After a few minutes, a groan escaped his lips. He put down the *tefillin* and began to put on the ordinary *tefillin.*

"Why aren't you putting on our father's *tefillin*?" The Sadgorer *rebbe* pretended to be surprised.

"I used to be able to sense their holiness, but now, because of my unworthiness, I don't feel it anymore," admitted Reb Dovid Moshe sorrowfully.

"You – unworthy?" protested Reb Avrohom Yaakov. "My dear brother, the reason you don't feel its holiness anymore is that the original *parshios* were removed and replaced with other ones. In fact, I have the original ones. Please don't ask me any questions, but just take them. Here you are." He handed his brother the stolen *batim*.

Reb Dovid Moshe's jaw dropped in amazement. He examined the *batim*. "Yes, these are our father's *parshios*," he said, recognizing them. "Now I understand why I have not been able to sense the *tefillin*'s holiness! It didn't have the real *parshios* in it," he exclaimed.

"My brother is amazing!" Reb Avrohom Yaakov realized. "He could actually feel that the holiness was gone! In his humility he assumed the reason was that he wasn't worthy."

Out of respect for his brother's wish, Reb Dovid Moshe did not ask any questions – to the relief of the two anxious youths who had come along.

From then on, Reb Dovid Moshe always carefully hid his *tefillin* after his morning prayers. And no one else ever knew where he concealed them.

Part 2

Many years went by. Reb Dovid Moshe moved from Potek to Chortkov and became *rebbe* there. The reputation of the Chortkover *rebbe*, as he was called, spread far and wide. Jews from all over flocked to his side to seek spiritual guidance and to receive his blessings.

When Reb Dovid Moshe was old, he sent for his only son,

Reb Yisroel. "I feel that my days on this earth are numbered," he said to his son. "I bequeath to you my most precious possession – the *tefillin* of my great-great-grandfather, the Mezhirecher *Magid*. Cherish it and guard it as you would the apple of your eye."

Reb Yisroel succeeded his father of blessed memory as the next Chortkover *rebbe*. He did indeed guard and protect the *tefillin* carefully. In fact, he had such awe of the *tefillin* that he wore it only twice a year – on Purim and on *erev* Yom Kippur.

But one sad day, Reb Yisroel and the *Magid's tefillin* were parted. It happened in this way. World War I had broken out. The Russian armies were invading Galicia and were coming close to Chortkov. Panic swept through the town. The inhabitants fled, afraid for their lives. Reb Yisroel panicked too. In his hurry to save his family, he forgot the precious *tefillin*.

Cossacks rode into Chortkov, pillaging and plundering wherever they went. Whatever was valuable they looted. The rest they smashed and broke. Then they set fire to the homes, Reb Yisroel's home among them.

Meanwhile the Chortkover *rebbe* and his family reached Lvov, intending to stay there until it was safe to return to their hometown. When word reached Reb Yisroel about the looting and burning of his home, he was heartsick. But what grieved him the most was the loss of his great-great-grandfather's *tefillin*. He could not put it out of his mind. "How could I have forgotten it?" he thought over and over remorsefully.

The cossacks conquered one city after the other. Now they were getting close to Lvov. Once again the family prepared to escape. This time they fled to Vienna, the capital city, to wait until the fury of war was over. The war, however, dragged on and got even worse.

One day the Chortkover *rebbe* got word that the Russians had been repulsed and were out of Galicia. The town of Chortkov was free once more. Reb Yisroel called a *chasid* and instructed him with a mission.

"Go to Chortkov," he said, "and see what condition the town is in. See if there is any possibility for us to return and rebuild our lives there. While you are there, please look for my *tefillin*. See if you can find it. You know how much it means to me."

The messenger departed. As it was wartime, traveling was slow and conditions dangerous. Several weeks went by during which Reb Yisroel waited, agonizing.

At last the messenger returned. The news was not good. "Most of the city is burned, and the *rebbe's* home and everything in it is destroyed. The small handful of Jews who have resettled there are destitute. It would not be advisable to return."

"And the *tefillin* – did you find it?" asked the *rebbe* anxiously.

"I searched all over. I asked around. Nobody knew anything about it. They said that probably it went up in flames with the other things," the *chasid* sorrowfully replied.

Though everyone else seemed to bear the news, the *rebbe* could not accept the fact that his beloved *tefillin* was lost forever. Every day when he donned his *tefillin*, he thought about it. On Purim and *erev* Yom Kippur – the days that he used to wear the special *tefillin* – he cried inconsolably. If only he hadn't forgotten it in his rush to leave Chortkov!

Part 3

One fine day after the long war finally ended, a Jewish soldier appeared at the door of Reb Yisroel's home. "I would like to have a word with the *rebbe*, he said to the *rebbe's gabai*.

The *gabai* looked at the soldier's torn and tattered uniform disdainfully. "The *rebbe* isn't seeing people right now. Come back later," he told the soldier.

The soldier would not leave, however. "I need to see the *rebbe* right now," he insisted. "It's urgent."

When the *gabai* realized how determined the soldier was, he said, "Let me see what the *rebbe* says."

The *gabai* went to the *rebbe* and informed him, "There is a Jewish soldier outside. He's from the Russian army. I told him that you are not receiving people now, but he insists that it's important."

The *rebbe* replied, "It's obviously an urgent matter. Tell him to come in."

The *gabai* went outside and led the soldier in to see the *rebbe*. The soldier entered the *rebbe*'s room. Without a word, he drew something out of his knapsack and placed it on the desk in front of the *rebbe*. It was the *tefillin*.

The *rebbe*'s heart skipped a beat.

"I found these *tefillin* in your house, *Rebbe*, and now I am returning them to you," the soldier explained.

The *rebbe* was so moved that he could not speak for a few minutes. Lovingly he picked up the long-lost *tefillin* and caressed them tenderly.

At last he spoke, his voice choked. "Tell me, young man, how did these *tefillin* come into your possession?"

"Let me tell you my story, *Rebbe*," the soldier responded. "I was born in Russia. When the war broke out, I joined the army. I was stationed near the Austrian border. We received orders to cross the border into Austria and raid the border towns. We crossed the border and had several skirmishes with Austrian soldiers. This situation lasted for several weeks.

"At last the fighting began in earnest. We were ordered to find and attack the Austrian troops, who had begun to flee. We marched after them but were unable to overtake them.

"En route we passed through the town of Chortkov. It had already been raided by a band of cossacks several days earlier. I had very special feelings about the town. When I was a child, my father had taken me to Chortkov, which was right across the border from Russia, to see the *rebbe*. The place is a terrible sight to behold now—burned-out buildings, doors broken in, windows shattered, furniture smashed. I had seen it in all its glory. It was very painful to see it now in ruins.

"The soldiers in my detachment rummaged through the debris to see if they could find anything of value. I followed them into the *rebbe*'s once stately residence. There were heaps of broken and partially burned household articles, and there were piles of holy books, many of them torn.

"I looked through the piles. There among the *seforim* I found a case with the *tefillin*. To my surprise they were completely intact and undamaged. Somehow they had miraculously escaped destruction.

"I said to myself, 'Let me take these *tefillin*. If with God's help I survive the war, I will bring them back to their rightful owner, the Chortkover *rebbe*.' I could tell the *tefillin* were special. I never used them. I put on my own *tefillin* every day.

"All through the long, miserable war, I kept them with me. They seemed to protect me. While all around me men fell in battle or died of starvation, I was never harmed. I felt somehow that I was saved each time in the merit of the *tefillin*.

"Wherever I went, I took the *tefillin* with me. One day I had a lucky break. I was captured by the enemy and placed in a prison camp, where I had food and where I did not have to fight. I watched over the *tefillin* there too, or I should say the *tefillin* watched over me. Fortunately, I remained there in the prison camp till the war was over. Then I set out to find you, *Rebbe*, and return the *tefillin* to you."

The soldier had finished his story.

"The *tefillin*, as you rightly guessed, are very special and holy *tefillin*," the *rebbe* explained. "They belonged to my great-great-great-grandfather, the *Magid* of Mezhirech. That is why nothing could harm them – neither cossacks nor fire nor destruction."

The *rebbe* continued, "And because you intended to do the *mitzvah* of returning a lost object to its owner, you were protected, for if one is on a mission to do a *mitzvah*, one is guarded from harm. May the angels of God, who watched over you throughout the war, continue to watch over you so that you return safely to your family and reunite with them."

Having observed the soldier's ragged garments, the *rebbe* wanted to give him some money with which to buy new clothes. He looked in his pockets but they were empty. The *rebbe* said to the young man, "One minute, please, I'll be right back." He went into the next room and got some money.

When the *rebbe* returned, the soldier was gone.

The *rebbe* hurried to the door to catch him. There was no soldier in sight. "Did you see the soldier leave?" he asked the *gabai*.

"No," answered the *gabai*. "I only saw him come in."

The *rebbe* looked everywhere but could not find him. No one had seen a man dressed in the uniform of a Russian soldier.

The *rebbe* asked a child playing on the street if he had seen anyone. "Yes, I saw a soldier leave the *rebbe*'s house and go down the street," he said.

The *rebbe* quickly sent messengers to look for the soldier in the streets, in the marketplace, in the *shuls*—all over. But the search proved fruitless. The soldier had vanished without a trace and was never seen again.

REB ZUSHA OF ANNOPOL

Born: ?
Died: 1800 (5560)
Lived in: Poland
Best known as: Younger brother of Reb Elimelech of Lyzhansk and for his humility and love of every creature

✳ 8 ✳

Reb Zusha and the Drunken Soldiers

What is all that noise?" wondered Yankel the innkeeper nervously.

Soldiers suddenly entered, pushing and shoving their way through the door. More and more came in, too many for Yankel to count.

"Give us booze!" yelled the soldiers. They were very excited because they had just won a battle. Yankel gave them vodka, but they did not pay. They just shouted for more. Soon Yankel was out of vodka. The drunken soldiers pounded on the tables. "More!" they yelled. But Yankel had no more. The soldiers had drunk up all his liquor. They became enraged and began hurling glasses to the floor and breaking chairs into smithereens.

Yankel stood helplessly by, watching the wild soldiers ransack his inn. "If you don't give us more booze, we'll break every bone in your body, and your children's, too," the soldiers threatened.

Poor Yankel was terrified. "I will run to the *rebbe* Reb Zusha. He will surely help me," thought Yankel.

Fear lent him wings, and Yankel sped straight to the *beis midrash*. There sat the *tzadik* Reb Zusha of Annopol, the *talmid* of the holy Mezhirecher *Magid*, deep in study.

"*Rebbe, Rebbe*, help me," Yankel pleaded. "Soldiers came into my inn and drank up everything, and now they are destroying the place. They want to beat me and my family up now, too."

The *rebbe* immediately put down his *sefer*. "Let's go there together right now," he declared.

Yankel and the *tzadik* hurried to the inn. Reb Zusha stood at the window, looking in at the soldiers as they wildly rampaged.

Reb Zusha uttered three words: *"Uv'chien tain pachdecho"* ("Put Your fear upon them").

Reb Zusha recited it again. He recited it a third time.

All at once, the soldiers stopped their rampaging and looked at the *tzadik*'s face in the window. They became very scared. Their teeth chattered, their knees trembled, and their hands shook.

"Let's get out of here!" they shrieked.

They rushed to the door, but they couldn't all fit through at the same time. They began jumping through the windows. Their fright did not leave them outside. Terrified, they kept running.

The general saw them running and wanted to know why. But he was unable to ask them anything because they scampered past him too fast. The general lost his temper. "I order you to stop running immediately!" he roared.

The soldiers stopped. With chattering teeth they explained, "There was a man at the window. He scared us. He kept repeating something very strange—*pachdecho* or something."

"What were you doing over there in the inn? Were you making trouble?" the general demanded. "About-face! On your march! Go straight back to the inn. I want to see what mischief you did there." The unhappy soldiers were forced to go back to the inn.

When the general saw what destruction the soldiers had

brought about, he said, "You soldiers will have to pay for all the damage you have done and for all the liquor you drank. You will also be punished for your inexcusably wild behavior."

In the end, Yankel was paid every penny that was owed him. Only then did the soldiers finally stop trembling. It goes without saying they never bothered Yankel after that.

Thus did the holy *tzadik*, the *rebbe* Reb Zusha, save a Jewish innkeeper from ruin. May his merit stand by us in good stead!

✳✳ 9 ✳✳

A Day in *Elul*

When the month of *Elul* rolls around, thoughts of *teshuvah* arise in the heart and mind of every Jew. The *rebbe* Reb Zusha would also search his heart and do penitence. If one listened carefully one might be able to hear the righteous man having the following conversation with himself.

"Zusha, Zusha," he would say to himself, "when are you going to do *teshuvah* already?"

"Today, Zusha!" Zusha would answer himself. "Today I am going to start doing *teshuvah*!"

"But Zusha," he would exclaim next, "you said the same thing yesterday!"

Then the holy man would sternly tell himself, "Oh, but *this* time I really mean it. Today I am *really* going to start doing *teshuvah*."

REB ELIMELECH OF LYZHANSK

Born:	1717 (5477)
Died:	1786 (5546)
Lived in:	Poland
His *rebbe*:	*Magid* of Mezhirech
Best known as:	The *rebbe* of many great Polish *rebbes*
Also called:	Noam Elimelech (for the book he wrote by that name)

❊❊ 10 ❊❊

The Strange Wedding Gifts

Shalom, the orphan lad, worked for Reb Aaron, or as some affectionately called him, Reb Ahre'le. Reb Ahre'le had an inn and a whiskey distillery, which he rented from the *poritz.* Every so often, Shalom went to the nearby town of Lyzhansk to buy supplies for Reb Ahre'le. Whenever he had extra time, he would go to see the *rebbe* Reb Elimelech, who lived in the town.

"*Rebbe*," the young Shalom would appeal to him, "I'm all on my own. I have no parents to take care of me. Bless me that I should find my right marriage partner, please!"

In the home of the saintly Reb Elimelech there lived a poor orphan girl by the name of Lieba. The *rebbe* and his wife were concerned about her welfare. "Perhaps," he suggested one day to Shalom, "you can find a job for Lieba at your place."

"As a matter of fact," remarked Shalom, "my boss is looking for a housekeeper. If she wants, she can have the job. She can come back with me when I return, if she likes."

Lieba was pleased with the idea. She quickly packed her things. The *rebbe* wished them *brochah v'hatzlochah*, and they left.

On their way to the village, Shalom gave the orphan girl a few tips. "Do what I do," he advised her. "Instead of taking your salary every two weeks, have Reb Ahre'le keep it for you. That way you'll be sure to save up a lot."

Lieba took Shalom's advice. For six months she worked and did not draw her salary, but let her boss keep it. Then, an unfortunate thing happened. At the end of six months, the innkeeper's business, which had been doing poorly for a while, failed completely. Reb Ahre'le lost all his money and his investments, including the investments of his employees. The two orphans were left without any money.

What a disappointment it was! But Shalom and Lieba didn't lose heart. They immediately began to look for another job. They soon found other jobs in which each of them would be paid fifty guldens a year.

Shalom and Lieba worked for twelve months at their new jobs. At the end of that time, Shalom suggested, "Let's get our wages and go find ourselves another position."

"Yes. We need to find a better job than this," Lieba agreed.

They collected their wages and prepared to leave. "I'm going to *shul* to *daven* before we leave," Shalom told her.

In a corner of the *shul* sat a beggar in ragged clothing. There was something familiar about the unfortunate man. Suddenly Shalom realized who it was.

"Reb Ahre'le!" he gasped in shock and disbelief.

"Yes, it's me," said Reb Ahre'le sadly. "I went broke. I have to beg for a living now."

Shalom could not believe how his former boss had changed. Reb Ahre'le's formerly healthy complexion was now worn and haggard; his once fine clothes were now in tatters. What had happened to the successful innkeeper Shalom had known and admired?

"Isn't there *any* way to pull yourself up again?" protesed the young man.

"I could do it one, two, three. All I need is one hundred guldens. With that I could buy myself a small business and stand on my own feet again," replied the beggar.

"One hundred guldens," thought Shalom. "That is exactly what Lieba and I have!"

Shalom hurried back to tell Lieba the news. "I saw Reb Ahre'le and he looks terrible. He has to beg to get food," Shalom reported.

Lieba was horrified to hear the shocking news.

"He says all he needs is one hundred guldens and he can get back on his feet," Shalom related. "Lieba, if we put our wages together, we can give him the one hundred guldens!"

"Yes, but that's all the money we own!" she retorted.

"So what?" answered Shalom. "We're young, strong, and healthy. We can find work and make some more money."

"That's fine for you to say," Lieba shot back. "But what about me? I'm not married. I'll be an old maid and penniless." Lieba thought for a while. Then she made up her mind. "I'll do it if you marry me."

Shalom was taken aback. He hadn't expected this. "Yes, perhaps we should get married! Why didn't I think of it myself?"

So Shalom collected their money and took it to Reb Ahre'le, who accepted it very thankfully. Reb Ahre'le would now be able to set himself up in business and, please God, prosper once again.

Shalom and Lieba, on the other hand, could not afford to get married just yet, as they had not a penny to their names. They went to work gathering wood in the forest and selling it in the town. For many days and weeks they worked until finally Shalom announced, "Now we can afford to get married."

On the *Shabbos* before Shalom and Lieba were to be married, the *rebbe* Reb Elimelech sat around the *shalosh seudos* table with his *talmidim*. Every *Shabbos* they would linger at the *shalosh seudos*, savoring and stretching the last hours of the *Shabbos*, but this week the Noam Elimelech made *Havdalah* quickly, as soon as the stars came out.

Then into the wagon climbed the *rebbe* and ten of his *talmidim*. They rode for a long, long time, until they were very far from their town of Lyzhansk. When the carriage finally halted at a crossroads before an inn, it was after midnight.

The inn was run by a Jewish innkeeper and was a favorite stopping place for Jewish travelers. Soon everyone at the inn that night found out that the *tzadik* Reb Elimelech had arrived. They all came out to greet him.

Among the lodgers at the inn were Shalom and Lieba, who were on their way back from the forest where they had been gathering wood. "Can you imagine? Reb Elimelech is here, at our inn!" Shalom joyfully reported to his fiancée. "It's been such a long time since I last saw him!"

"The *rebbe*?" Lieba clapped her hands excitedly. "Why, he was like a father to me! Let's go tell him about our wedding tomorrow."

When the *rebbe* heard of their plans, he said, "My children, why don't you get married tonight? I would very much like to be at your *chasunah*." Why not, indeed? What could be nicer than to have their beloved *rebbe* be *mesader kidushin* at their wedding and his holy *talmidim* be their wedding guests?

The innkeeper was willing to cook the food for the *simchah*. "I always have plenty of food on hand, so it's no problem," he told them.

The bride and groom did not have their wedding clothes

with them, but the hotel guests happily lent them their finest clothes.

The celebration got under way with dancing and merriment. Everyone was delighted to be sharing in the *simchah* of the two orphans. Suddenly the *rebbe* indicated that he would like to speak. All the guests grew silent.

"It is time to give the *choson* and *kallah* their wedding presents," he announced, with a twinkle in his eye. "My wedding gift to the young couple is this village."

The village his wedding gift? What could the saintly man possibly mean?

A *talmid* of the Noam Elimelech presented his gift next. "My present to Shalom and Lieba is the water mill in the neighboring village."

The water mill? It sounded nice enough. But what did it mean?

Next, another student announced his *chasunah geshenk.* "I am giving them a thousand golden ducats," he declared.

"And I'm giving them another thousand ducats," added another *talmid.*

Neither the *choson,* the *kallah,* the innkeeper, nor any of the guests could fathom what was the meaning of the strange *chasunah geshenk* of the *rebbe* and his disciples.

After the *Birkas HaMazon* and the *Sheva Brochos* were over, the Noam Elimelech blessed the new couple, and he and his *chevrah* boarded their carriage again and left.

The next day Shalom and Lieba went out as usual to work in the woods. When they reached the densest part of the forest, they heard the sound of someone moaning weakly. They followed the sound till they reached a swampy area. A young man had sunk in up to his chest in the soft, oozing mud.

"Help me!" he begged feebly. "I'm sinking, and I'm so weak I can't fight anymore."

"We'll help you," Shalom answered him in a soothing voice. "You'll be out of there in just a few minutes."

Without wasting a moment, Shalom formed a rope out of his and Lieba's jackets. He threw it to the sinking man, who caught it in his hands. Then Shalom and Lieba pulled at the rope with all their might, straining every muscle of their bodies. A couple of times Shalom almost lost his footing and nearly slipped into the treacherous mud himself. Finally, they succeeded in freeing the man from the swamp. He was exhausted from the ordeal.

Gratefully, the young man murmured, "Thank you for saving my life."

"Who are you?" Shalom and Lieba asked curiously. "What brought you to this forsaken part of the forest? And how did you get sucked up into this treacherous swamp?"

"My name is Georg," replied the young man. "My father is the squire of this district. Yesterday I was supposed to get married. I thought I would sneak out into the forest, catch an animal, and bring it back to surprise everyone. But while I was hunting, I fell into this swamp. That was over twelve hours ago. I struggled for most of the time, but the more I struggled, the deeper I sank. It's good you found me when you did because I was getting very weak and soon I would have sunk in all the way."

Shalom and Lieba helped the worn-out young man walk back to their inn, where they fed him leftovers from their wedding the night before. Then they assisted him into their wagon and drove him to the castle of his father, the squire.

How happy and relieved Georg's family was to see him!

The family had been sick with worry and fear. All the friends and relatives who had assembled for the wedding were still there, too, anxiously waiting for some news of the missing bridegroom.

"Oh, Georg!" cried his parents, embracing their son. "You're alive! We looked all over for you! We were afraid that the worst had happened! Where were you?"

So Georg related the whole story to his family and friends. When he told them how Shalom and Lieba had rescued him, the squire and his wife thanked the young couple with tears of gratitude in their eyes.

"How can we reward these wonderful people properly?" asked the squire. "I, for one, shall give them the village as a present."

"And I," exclaimed Georg's mother gratefully, "give them a present of a thousand golden ducats as a token of appreciation."

"To show them how thankful I am, I'll give them the water mill in my village," said Georg's father-in-law.

"And," added Georg's mother-in-law, "I will give them another thousand ducats of my own."

Shalom and Lieba were now a very wealthy young couple. God had rewarded them measure for measure for the self-sacrifice they had displayed in helping their former employer.

Thus were the blessings of the *tzadik* Reb Elimelech and his holy disciples fulfilled.

REB YECHIEL MICHEL OF ZLOTSHOV

Born:	1721 (5481)
Died:	1786 (5546)
Lived in:	Galicia
His *rebbes*:	Baal Shem Tov; the *Magid* of Mezhirech
His successors:	Each of his five sons, who became *rebbes*

✼ 11 ✼

The Amulet

Part 1

In the time that Reb Yechiel Michel was *rebbe* in Zlotshov, there lived in a nearby village a Jewish innkeeper and his family. The innkeeper was very poor. He owed many months of rent to the *poritz*, who was a mean and vicious nobleman.

The nobleman appeared before the innkeeper, roaring "I demand that you pay me right now all that you owe me."

"I don't have the money just now," quavered the innkeeper. "Can you wait a little bit? Perhaps I'll have some of it for you in a month or so."

"Impossible," the nobleman snarled in disgust. "I've waited three years and that's long enough. I'm going to throw you all into the dungeon—you, your wife, and your children. At least there I'll get some use out of you. You'll grind the mill in the dungeon for the rest of your miserable lives."

"Have mercy on my small children!" pleaded the innkeeper. "I'll get you the money somehow."

But the nobleman was pitiless. "Cast them into the dungeon!" he bellowed to his servants.

The unfortunate innkeeper and his family were thrown into the cold, bleak dungeon. There they had to work at the mill. They were given very little to eat, and the light of day never penetrated their cell.

"Will we be imprisoned forever? Will there ever be an end to our backbreaking labor?" The family prayed to God to rescue them from their suffering.

After a few months, the innkeeper's wife gave birth to a baby boy. "How will we give our baby a *bris milah*? He must have one on the eighth day." Husband and wife agonized over their problem.

Somehow the Jewish community heard about the innkeeper's problem. They sent a delegation of important people to the nobleman. "Please give the innkeeper and his family permission to leave the pit and have a *bris* for their newborn son," they asked.

Grudgingly he gave his permission. "But there'll be guards there. Don't let them try any monkey business," the nobleman warned.

On the eighth day of the baby's life, the family emerged from their prison. It was the first time they had seen sunlight since the beginning of their captivity. The circumcision took place and everyone sat down to eat the meal.

The guards sat down to eat, too. They helped themselves generously to the vodka there. Soon they were all drunk.

The village mayor attended as well. Seeing the plight of the innkeeper and his family, his heart softened. "I have an offer to make to you," he whispered to the innkeeper. "For a few rubles, I'll get you out of here."

The innkeeper's heart leaped. "But how?" he asked, bewildered.

"I have three horses that can run like the wind. We can cover forty miles in one night. By the time the nobleman realizes you're gone, we'll be far away from here."

The innkeeper was doubtful. "But he'll send his men after us to catch us! And if they catch us, the *poritz* will have no mercy on us. He'll kill us for sure."

"Don't worry. He won't know which road to take. Besides, the roads are icy and his men won't get far," the mayor encouraged him.

The innkeeper made his decision. "I accept your offer." He paid the mayor the money.

"But we must leave immediately. We don't have a second to spare," the mayor urged.

The innkeeper quickly rounded up his family. Hurriedly, they mounted the horses. The horses took off like the wind.

After they had gone thirty miles, the mayor let the horses stop to rest a little.

"Do you have the baby?" the innkeeper's wife asked.

"No, I don't. I thought you had him!" the innkeeper cried out sharply.

"My baby!" wailed the distraught mother. "Mayor, turn the horses around immediately. We must go back and get our baby."

"We can't go back!" snapped the mayor. "If we do, we'll all be killed."

So they went on, the grief-stricken family weeping bitterly all the rest of the way.

At last they stopped at a village far away from the nobleman's village. Here they would be safe from the clutches of the nobleman.

Meanwhile back at the nobleman's village, the guards woke up from their drunken stupor. They blinked their eyes and looked around. Nobody was there. "The prisoners—they're gone!" they gasped.

They informed the nobleman, fearful of his wrath.

He exploded in a roar. "Get on your horses right now and look for them," he shouted. "You had better catch them!"

The night was very cold, the streets were icy, and several hours had already passed since the prisoners' escape. The guards searched the roads but did not find them. They gave up.

Upon their return, they heard a baby crying. "Oh, look! The prisoners forgot their baby!" they exclaimed in surprise.

When the nobleman saw the baby, he growled, "Well, at least I have one of them. I'll make a slave out of him."

The mayor, who had meanwhile returned, showed up. No one suspected him of having anything to do with the prisoners' escape. "Please let me have this baby," he begged the nobleman. "My wife and I have no children of our own, and we would love to keep this child."

The nobleman, who really had no love for infants, agreed. "You can have the sniveling thing!" he snorted.

The mayor and his wife were delighted. They took the baby into their home and raised him with all the luxuries they could afford. As the child was quite intelligent, his adoptive father entrusted him with watching the sheep when he was still quite young. Once, when he was eight years old, the child quarreled with the other shepherd boys. "You think you're so great just because your father is the mayor," they taunted him. "Well, we have news for you. He's not really your father."

"What?" The boy turned white.

"That's right. He's not your father. And you're not even Polish. You're Jewish," they jeered.

"What are you talking about?" gasped the boy.

"Your father was a Jewish innkeeper who was in jail and escaped. The mayor and his wife merely raised you."

"I don't believe you!" the boy protested.

"Then how come you're circumcised and we're not?!" they retorted.

The boy walked home, thunderstruck. "I'm Jewish," he whispered to himself over and over. "My parents are Jewish. I want to be a Jew like them." The boy, whose name was David, did not stop thinking about his newfound Jewishness. "I must run away and find my people," was all he could think about.

Finally, when the mayor and his wife went away on a long trip, David saw his chance to run away. He fled to the city. There he found a Jewish person to whom he told his story.

The Jewish community took the boy under its wing. They fed him and gave him a place to stay. They took away his old clothes, which were made of *shatnes* – linen and wool – and gave him new clothes and a *tallis koton*. They taught him the *alef-beis* and how to read and pray.

Worried that the mayor might come looking for the runaway boy, the community sent David to a city farther away. There David began learning *Chumash*. An apt and eager student, he caught on quickly. He began to study Talmud. After his *bar mitzvah*, he was sent to a *yeshivah*. In the course of time, David was asked to teach the younger boys.

Part 2

Eventually David was hired by a Jewish family as a private tutor for their children. David went to live with the new family and be the children's teacher.

One time, David's boss was getting ready for a trip. "I am going to Zlotshov to my *rebbe*, the holy Reb Michel. Would you care to come with me?" he offered David.

"I would love to go." David's eyes sparkled. "Perhaps the *rebbe* can tell me where my father and mother are."

David and his boss arrived in Zlotshov. David waited in line to see the holy *tzadik*. He related his life story to the saintly teacher. When David finished, Reb Michel wrote some words on a piece of parchment, wrapped a scrap of leather around it, and sewed it up. Handing it to the young man, the *rebbe* instructed him, "Wear this amulet around your neck at all times. Don't open it until you get married. Then, when you are standing under the *chupah*, give the amulet to the *rav*, who will open it and read it. Do not go on with the *chupah* until he reads it. Will you do as I say?"

"Yes, I will," promised David. He put the amulet around his neck and from that time on wore it constantly.

Shortly after his return from Zlotshov, David went to work for a new family in another town, far away. He was nineteen then, the age at which boys got married at that time. David's new employer had a wealthy business friend who visited from time to time. The friend noticed the young tutor and took a liking to him.

One day the rich man spoke to David and asked him, "Would you be interested in a *shiduch* with my daughter? She is, if I may say so myself, a lovely girl. I think the two of you would make a wonderful pair."

"Yes, I would like to meet her," agreed David. The rich man took David to his village some twelve miles distant to meet his daughter. The two young people met and found each other agreeable. The couple was engaged and a date was set for the wedding. Meanwhile David continued working.

When the wedding day drew near, David went to the village of his bride, accompanied by his employer. They were greeted joyfully by the bride's family. All the preparations had been made. The *chupah* had already been erected. The wedding was about to take place.

At that moment, the bridegroom suddenly remembered the Zlotshover *rebbe*'s instructions.

"We need a *rav*," David announced.

"Why?" the bride and her parents protested.

David replied, "The *rebbe* said that a *rav* must read my amulet before the *chasunah* takes place."

The bride's father sent to the nearest city for a *rav*. The next day a *rav* arrived. Once more the guests assembled and the *chupah* was set up again. The *choson* removed the leather packet from his neck and gave it to the *rav*.

The *rav* undid the binding and unrolled the parchment. On it was written one short sentence: "May a brother marry his sister?"

The *rav* wrinkled his brow in puzzlement. "I have no idea what this means. Here," he said to David, "please read it. Perhaps you will understand it."

David looked at it, and all at once his face lit up with joy. He shouted with glee. He jumped up into the air and danced exuberantly around the room, all the while crying tears of happiness.

The bride's parents were stunned. "Has the bridegroom gone crazy?" they wondered.

The *rav* took David into another room. He asked him, "Why have these six little words made you go wild with joy?"

David took a deep breath and tried to relax. "I'll explain it all to you," he said to the *rav*.

David told him how he had been separated from his family as a baby. "This must be my long-lost family," concluded David.

The *rav* did not know what to think. He called in the bride's parents and began interrogating them. "Where do you originally come from?" he asked.

They told him the name of the *shtetl* where they originally came from.

"And what happened there?" he continued.

"We were thrown into a dungeon because of our debts, but with God's help we escaped."

"All of you?"

"No. We left our baby boy behind."

"How many years ago was that?"

"Nineteen years ago."

"I'm nineteen years old," cried David. "I'm your son! You're my parents! The *kallah* is my sister!"

"No, it couldn't be." The family shook their heads in disbelief.

"I'll tell you the nobleman's name. Will you believe me then?" David told them the name of the nobleman. "I'll tell you the name of the mayor who helped you escape and who raised me till I was eight." He told them that too.

Finally they believed him. What a reunion there was! Parents and son, sisters and brothers fell on each other's necks and laughed and cried! They hugged and embraced one another. They thanked God for reuniting them after all the years. Such happiness there was! Their joy knew no bounds. No wedding could ever have been as jubilant as this reunion.

Only then did David appreciate the prophetic vision of the *tzadik* Reb Michel. And only then did he realize the terrible sin that would have resulted – a brother marrying his sister – if not for those six little words written by the *rebbe* on that amulet.

✳✳ 12 ✳✳

The *Kichel* on the Bookcase

R eb Michel of Zlotshov knew the taste of poverty. He could see it everywhere he turned. In his children's worn and patched clothes. In their gaunt and pinched faces. In the ramshackle hut he lived in. But the more his stomach rumbled with the pangs of hunger, the more zealously Reb Michel studied Torah. And when he put his heart and soul into his studies, he would forget everything else – his poverty, his family's misery, and all his troubles.

One day there was nothing to eat in the house. Reb Michel's son Yossele was so hungry that he cried himself to sleep. The next day the child awoke, faint with hunger.

"Tati," he whimpered, "I'm so weak. It feels as if my *neshamah* is leaving me."

"What?" cried his father in alarm. "Don't say that! I'm sure we can find some food somewhere. In fact, I think I remember seeing a *kichel* on top of the bookcase."

"Really, Tati?" Yossele perked up. He dragged a chair over to the bookcase and climbed up to reach the top shelf. To his delight he found the *kichel* there, just as his father had said.

Tightly clutching his newfound treasure, Yossele went and sat down in a corner. He made the *brochah* and took a bite out of the *kichel*. Slowly he consumed it, savoring every bite to the last morsel. When he had finished, he heaved a long sigh of satisfaction.

"I feel so much better, Tati, now that I have eaten that *kichel*," Yossele said. "But there's something I don't understand."

"What is puzzling you, my son?" his father asked, tenderly stroking his son's cheeks.

"Father," wondered Yossele, "why didn't you tell me about the *kichel* yesterday? You knew how hungry I was!"

Reb Michel pondered the question for a moment. "My dear Yossele, until a few minutes ago, I had completely forgotten about that *kichel*. But when you told me that you felt your *neshamah* leaving you, I knew God would never let it come to such a predicament. Surely there must be a way out! And at that moment I suddenly remembered."

"You mean we should never lose hope, even when things look very bad?" his son asked.

"You're a clever boy, my son. That is right. And now you must let your father resume his studies." And Reb Michel once more delved into the holy books of the Torah.

The little Yossele grew up to be the *tzadik* Reb Yossi of Yampule, of blessed memory.

❊❊ 13 ❊❊

Tefillin for an *Esrog*

The *rebbe* Reb Yechiel Michel of Zlotshov was so poor that often the family went hungry.

From time to time, Reb Michel's wife would plead with him. "Michel," she would say, "why don't you sell your father's *tefillin*? You don't use it anyway. You have your own *tefillin*. We could probably get fifty *reinish* for it! Think of how much food we can buy for the children with that money!"

But Reb Michel wouldn't hear of it. "Sell the only thing of value that I inherited from my holy father, Reb Yitzchak Drohobitcher, of blessed memory? I could never do that!"

But there came a day that Reb Michel finally did sell the treasured *tefillin* – only it wasn't to buy food for his family. This is what happened.

The holiday of Sukkos was fast approaching, and Reb Michel was very worried. Nowhere could an *esrog* be found! Not in the whole town of Zlotshov, nor anywhere in the vicinity.

On *erev* Sukkos, Reb Michel heard good news. Someone had an *esrog* for sale. It was a perfect *esrog*. The color was good, it had the right shape, there were no blemishes, and everything about it conformed to the requirements of the *Shulchan Aruch*.

"How much does he want for his *esrog*?" inquired Reb Michel.

"Fifty *reinish*," he was told.

Fifty *reinish* was exactly how much his father's *tefillin* was worth.

"It's a deal!" cried Reb Michel. He sold his precious inheritance and with the money bought the *esrog*.

He gazed at it delightedly. It was truly a flawless *esrog*. Now he would be able to perform the *mitzvah* of *lulav* and *esrog* properly.

When Reb Michel's wife saw the *esrog*, she became suspicious. "This is a lovely *esrog*," she said. "It must have cost quite a bit of money. How did you pay for it?"

"I sold the *tefillin*," Reb Michel reluctantly confessed.

"You sold the *tefillin*? For your hungry children you wouldn't sell it, but for a onetime *mitzvah* you sold it?" Her voice rose to a sharp fury. She grabbed the *esrog* and in her rage bit off the stem with her teeth.

The *esrog* was invalid. It could not be used.

What a bitter blow for Reb Michel! Now he had neither his precious *tefillin* nor an *esrog* for Sukkos. "If this is God's will, I accept it. I will not get angry at my wife. That would be very wrong." He did not utter one word of rebuke to his wife.

That night, Reb Michel's father appeared to him in a dream.

"My son," said the *tzadik* Reb Yitzchak Drohobitcher, "you showed great self-sacrifice by selling the *tefillin* for a *mitzvah* that you would use only seven days, but by not getting angry at your wife, you did a far greater and nobler deed. Up in heaven, the angels rejoiced when you restrained yourself and kept *shalom* in your home."

REB ARYEH LEIB OF SHPOLA

Born:	1725 (5435)
Died:	1811 (5572)
Lived in:	The Ukraine
His *rebbes*:	Baal Shem Tov, Reb Pinchas of Korets
Best known for:	Wandering from place to place helping Jews in need
Also called:	Shpoler *Zeide*

✳ 14 ✳

Everything Happens for a Reason

A *chasid* once appeared before the Shpoler *Zeide*, very upset. "*Rebbe,* I have a problem," he blurted out.

"What is it, my friend?" asked the Shpoler *Zeide,* concerned.

"Stolen goods were found on my land, and I'm being accused of stealing them and putting them there, but I didn't do anything. I never saw the items before. I have hired a lawyer to defend me in court, but he says the lightest sentence I could get is three months in jail."

"I'll be your lawyer before heaven and pray that your prison sentence should be no more than one month," the *rebbe* answered him encouragingly.

"But why should I go to jail for even one month? I'm innocent! I didn't do anything! It's just not fair."

The *Zeide* tried to comfort him. "The same thing once happened to me years ago," he said. "I was sentenced to two months in prison for something I didn't do. But I didn't complain."

"You didn't?" The Jew was taken aback. "Why not?"

"Because I knew that there must be a good reason for it," explained the *tzadik.*

"And was there a good reason?" inquired the Jew.

"There certainly was," affirmed the *Zeide*. "Let me tell you what happened."

The Shpoler *Zeide*'s Story

Once I spent *Shabbos* in an inn in a village near Poltava. There was another guest there at the same time who appeared to be a bit of a scholar. A scholar he might have been, but God-fearing he was not, as it turned out.

We left together, the other guest and I, early Sunday morning. He kept turning around, looking back at the village, but I had no idea what he was looking for. Suddenly, a carriage could be seen approaching us from the direction of the village.

The other man turned to me and asked, "Would you mind watching my suitcase for a few minutes? I'll be back soon." And he disappeared into the woods. I waited for him to return. Meanwhile the carriage had drawn up where I was sitting on the roadside. Two men jumped down from the wagon. One was the innkeeper, the other the sheriff.

The innkeeper hollered, "That's the thief!"

They grabbed both suitcases and went through them. Pulling out silver spoons and a wine cup, the innkeeper triumphantly declared, "Here are the things he stole!"

The sheriff smacked me on the face. "So that's how you repay someone's hospitality!"

I was too stunned to say a word. They tied my hands and feet and threw me into the carriage. After a while, my mind cleared and I understood what had happened. "It wasn't I who stole it," I explained. "The other man did it. When he saw your carriage coming, he left his suitcase with me and disappeared. I did not steal the silver."

They laughed mockingly. "So you can talk after all. You tell some pretty good stories." One of them gave me a vicious kick in my side.

After that I didn't say anything. I only whispered a little prayer to God. "I accept Your judgment, God," I said.

In Poltava I was handed over to the police. They threw me into jail and locked me up in a room with hard-core criminals, murderers, and thieves. In the morning, I found myself surrounded by a gang of vicious-looking inmates.

"Well, look what we have here!" they jeered. "A Jewish prisoner! Well, well!"

"Tell him the rules!" yelled another one.

The fiercest-looking prisoner faced me, his arms akimbo, and loudly proclaimed, "Every new inmate has to pay to join our gang. Otherwise we can't guarantee your safety."

"I have no money," I told them. "The police took everything of mine. Anyway, I don't want to belong to a gang of thieves. I never stole anything in my life."

They didn't like my answer. One of the prisoners grabbed my beard and another one my *payos*. Tears of pain and humiliation sprang to my eyes. "Master of the Universe," I prayed, "please don't let me fall into the hands of these scoundrels!"

When they realized I was praying, they tormented me even more. "Let's take him to 'court,' " they proposed.

Three of the prisoners were appointed as judges. They passed their verdict: Whoever doesn't pay has to get beaten.

They dragged me onto a long bench and stretched me out on it. One prisoner held down my head and another my feet so that I couldn't move.

One of the "judges" was given the honor of striking me first. He struck me once. Suddenly he cried out, "My arm! My arm!"

"What's the matter?" the other prisoners asked in alarm.

"My arm is killing me," he moaned. "Owww."

His arm had swollen to many times its normal size. The skin was falling off in patches, and the blood underneath was flowing out freely.

"Help me!" groaned the prisoner. "Save me! I'm in terrible pain!"

The prisoners shouted for the wardens. Soon the prisoner was carried off to a hospital. I was forgotten for the moment, to my great relief.

After a while, I noticed the prisoners glancing at me and whispering. One said, "He must be a sorcerer."

Another one disagreed. "No. He's a holy man. We'd better leave him alone."

They didn't start up with me again after that. In fact, they began treating me quite respectfully. They even called me "Rabbi." When I prayed they would silently watch me in awe.

One of the prisoners there interested me. Everyone referred to him as "the gypsy." He was serving time in jail for stealing a horse. The other prisoners told me, though, that he really wasn't a gypsy but a Jew.

"Aha! So this must be the reason for my being here," I said to myself.

I befriended the gypsy. He told me his story. He had been orphaned as a young child. Until he was thirteen, the Jewish community took care of him. After that he went to work for a wagon driver, who taught him about horses. He met a band of gypsy horse dealers and became a part of their group, eating with them, wearing gypsy clothes, and calling himself a gypsy. Finally, a year before, he had been caught stealing a horse and sentenced to two years in prison.

I talked to him for many hours. I reminded him of his Jewish past, of the heritage he had forsaken. I spoke to him from the depths of my heart, and something seemed to awaken in him.

One morning he woke up quite shaken. I asked him, "What's the matter?"

"My parents came to me in a dream last night and warned me that I must listen to you and do whatever you tell me."

My friend listened to me more attentively after that. I taught him how to say the *Shma*. I taught him about *tefillin*. I cautioned him against eating forbidden foods. I advised him to pray to God to ask His forgiveness for all his past transgressions.

So every night, when the other prisoners were fast asleep, he would pray with great feeling and emotion, begging God to forgive him for having forsaken the Jewish way of life.

Two months went by. As I slept one night, Elijah the Prophet appeared to me in a dream. "It's time to leave the jail," he said. "Don't be afraid. When you get out, go the city of Zlotopoli and become a *shammes* there."

I woke up in a cold sweat. Putting all my trust in God, I took my suitcase and started to go. Then I remembered my friend, the *baal teshuvah*. How could I abandon him? If God could take me out of prison, why couldn't He take my friend too?"

Quietly I woke my friend up. "We're going to leave," I whispered into his ear. "Hold my belt and follow me."

The *baal teshuvah* did as I told him. We came to the first door. It was open. The guard was fast asleep. We went through the door and tiptoed onward. Every door we came to was open!

We reached the gate. The guard at the gate was snoring loudly. We passed through the gate. We were free men again!

All night long we walked, hoping that we were going in the direction of Zlotopoli, where Elijah had commanded me to go. When dawn broke, we passed through a village. We asked a Jewish person there, "Is this the right way to Zlotopoli?"

"Yes, it is," he said.

"May we rest here for a while?" I asked him. "We have walked all night."

The villager let us into his home, where we rested our weary bones.

After a few hours, we continued on our way. We walked for three days. At last we arrived at Zlotopoli. I immediately applied for the job of *shammes* of the *shul* and was given the job. I helped the *baal teshuvah* to find a job in another city.

"That's the end of my story," the Shpoler *Zeide* concluded. "So you see, don't feel bad if you have to go to jail for one month. There is a reason for everything that happens. Everything God does is for the good."

REB PINCHAS OF KORETS

Born:	1726 (5486)
Died:	1791 (5551)
Lived in:	Korets in Volhynia
His *rebbe*:	Baal Shem Tov
Best known as:	One of the greatest of the Baal Shem Tov's disciples

✳ 15 ✳

A Change of Heart

ll day long people streamed in and out of the home of Reb Pinchas of Korets and waited in long lines to see him. One after the other they poured out their woes to the *tzadik*.

"Reb Pinchas," lamented one, "my business is failing and my debts are growing. Bless me that my *parnosoh* should improve."

A woman pleaded, "My husband and I have been married five years and we have no children. Give us a *brochah* that we should have children."

"*Rebbe*," confessed another, "I sinned and I feel very bad about it. How can I atone for my sin?"

A couple came in crying. "Our daughter is very sick. Please *daven* for her so she may get well."

From one *Shabbos* to the next, Reb Pinchas answered questions, offered guidance, gave encouragement, advice, and blessings. He never had a moment's rest.

"When am I ever going to have time to serve God? When will I be able to study Torah and *daven* at my own pace?" Reb Pinchas moaned. "I just want to be left alone!"

Finally, one day, he could not stand it anymore. "Master of the Universe," he cried out, "I wish to dedicate my life totally to worshiping You. Please make people hate me. Then they won't bother me anymore!"

Since Reb Pinchas was a saintly man, his wish was fulfilled. From that moment on, Reb Pinchas Koretser was shunned by his fellow man. No one spoke to him. No one would have anything more to do with him. Reb Pinchas was left completely alone, just as he had wished. The only time during the day that the *tzadik* saw other people was when he was in *shul*, *davening* with the congregation.

The holiday of Sukkos was coming up, and Reb Pinchas needed someone to build his *sukkah* for him.

"Will you do me the kindness to help me put up my *sukkah*?" Reb Pinchas inquired of someone he knew.

"I can't, I'm too busy," was the reply he got.

Reb Pinchas asked someone else. "I'll pay you for your time," he added.

"I'm sorry, I won't be able to," the man answered. No one liked him and everyone found an excuse not to help him. Reb Pinchas felt bad, but he knew it was because of his own prayer that people disliked him.

At last he got a Russian to build the *sukkah*. "Fine, but I'll need some tools," the Russian informed him.

Reb Pinchas's wife asked their neighbor if she could borrow some tools.

"Oh, it's you," sneered the neighbor when she saw it was Reb Pinchas's wife. "We don't lend out our tools to anyone."

One after the other, people refused to lend her tools because they despised her husband. At last, someone relented and gave her the tools she needed.

Reb Pinchas breathed a sigh of relief to see his *sukkah* finally up.

It was the first night of Sukkos. The evening prayers were

over. Reb Pinchas cast his eyes around the *shul* for a guest to invite to his *yom tov* table. But no one was willing to go to his home, and so he went home alone.

He and his wife sat down to their *yom tov* meal alone. *"Leiyol Avrohom,"* Reb Pinchas said, uttering the prayer inviting the patriarch Avrohom, the first of the Sukkos *Ushpizin,* or guests, to come in. Reb Pinchas looked out the door and saw our father Avrohom standing outside his *sukkah,* unwilling to enter. "Please come into my *sukkah,"* entreated Reb Pinchas.

The patriarch replied, "It is not my custom to come into a *sukkah* where there are no guests."

Reb Pinchas was hurt to the quick. Rejected by the patriarch Avrohom, too? This was too much! "Oh, God," burst out the *tzadik.* "I can't bear it anymore. I take back my wish. Please let people like me as they used to!"

Because Reb Pinchas Koretser was a holy man, God accepted this prayer too. So once more, Reb Pinchas was beloved and sought after by droves of people. But he never again complained about it.

REB ARYEH LEIB SARAH'S

Born:	1730 (5490)
Died:	1791 (5551)
Lived in:	Volhynia
His *rebbes*:	Baal Shem Tov and the Mezhirecher *Magid*
Best known for:	Being involved in ransoming Jewish prisoners

✸✸ 16 ✸✸

The Tenth Man

eb Leib Sarah's used to travel around the countryside finding Jews in trouble and helping them. Once he was traveling before Yom Kippur, when he was caught in a storm. The very heavens seemed to open up and empty out buckets of rain on the earth. To Reb Leib's chagrin, he realized that he would not reach the city before Yom Kippur.

There was, however, a village nearby. With difficulty the *rebbe* was able to reach the village. He found a Jewish villager and asked him, "Will there be a *minyan* here for Yom Kippur?"

"There are eight Jewish people living right here in the village. Two other people who live in the nearby woods said they would come. So we should have a *minyan*," replied the villager.

Reb Leib heaved a sigh of relief.

Erev Yom Kippur the *tzadik* immersed himself in the nearby river. He ate the last meal before the fast and hurried to the little *shul.* While he was engrossed in prayers, the rest of the *minyan* arrived.

The sun was getting lower in the sky. Soon it would be time to say the most awesome prayer of the year – *Kol Nidrei.*

But when they counted each other, they realized that they

didn't have a *minyan*. The two people who lived in the woods weren't there. They soon got word that the two men had been arrested on a false charge and were being held in jail. That meant they had, counting Reb Leib, only nine people.

"Think hard, my friends," Reb Leib urged the villagers. "Are there no other Jews in the vicinity?"

"No. We know all the Jews here. There are no others," they told him.

"What about an apostate—a Jew who converted—God forbid—to Christianity? Are there any such Jews here?" Reb Leib persisted.

The villagers stared at the *tzadik*. "An apostate? Yes, there is one," they admitted fearfully. "The *poritz* is a Jewish apostate. Forty years ago the daughter of the previous *poritz* fell in love with him and begged her father to get him to marry her. Her father told him that if he gave up his Judaism and converted to Christianity, he would give him his daughter as a wife and all his property as his inheritance. The man accepted the offer and married her."

"I'm going to ask him to be our tenth man," Reb Leib declared.

"No, no! He'll never agree. He'll get angry and take it out on us." They tried to dissuade the *tzadik* from going.

But the *tzadik* would not be dissuaded. "It's okay. He won't get angry. Don't worry," he reassured them. "Please show me where he lives."

Taking off his *tallis*, enclothed in his white *kittel*, he strode toward the mansion of the *poritz*. He went quickly, as the sun was almost setting. He knocked on the door of the mansion. No one answered. Reb Leib didn't wait but opened the door and walked right in. There stood the *poritz*, who gaped at his visitor in wonderment. Reb Leib was truly an awesome sight, with his countenance radiating holiness, his snow-white *kittel* enveloping him, and a white hat upon his head.

They faced each other wordlessly. For a second, the thought occurred to the *poritz*, "I can throw this man to the dogs." But he did not move.

At last, Reb Leib broke the silence. "My mother, Sara, was a saintly woman," he began. "When she was a young girl, a son of the *poritz* saw her and wanted to marry her. He promised her a life of wealth and riches. She refused. To get out of his clutches, she married an old Jewish teacher. That man was my father. She passed the test that heaven had given her. But you—you did not pass your test."

The *poritz* did not say a word. He just stood and stared at the saintly man.

"It's not too late, though. The gates of *teshuvah* are always open. And what better time than now to do it—on Yom Kippur?"

Still the *poritz* did not move. The villagers began to think Reb Leib had made a terrible mistake and that they would suffer for it. Reb Leib tried again. "We are nine men. We need you for a tenth man."

The *poritz* finally spoke. "I'll come," he blurted in a choking voice.

Reb Leib entered the *shul* followed by the *poritz*. The *poritz* did not look right or left. He was given a *tallis*. Wordlessly he wrapped himself in it. He covered his face and head with the *tallis* so that none of his body could be seen.

Out of the ark Reb Leib withdrew two Torah scrolls. One he gave to the elder of the village, the other to the *poritz*. They stood on either side of Reb Leib as he recited the prayer that comes before *Kol Nidrei*. "With the permission of God and with the permission of the congregation, we are allowed to pray with the apostates."

When the *poritz* heard that, he groaned so loudly the villagers thought he would faint. But the *poritz* didn't move. He stood like a statue in the same place throughout the evening prayers. The next day he stood there too, unmoving, unseeing. He did not say anything. He did not even pray. He only cried. He cried so hard that his body shook. His *tallis* grew wet from the tears. When the confessionary prayer *Al Chet* was said, the *poritz* heaved great groans. He moaned with a sound that came from the depths of his heart, that sent a shudder throughout those present.

The end of the Day of Atonement was nearing. The congregation prayed the *Neila* prayer as the sun descended through the treetops. It was time to say the *Shma Yisroel*. The villagers watched, their eyes wide, as the *poritz*–a *poritz* no longer, but a Jew–walked to the open ark and embraced the Torah scrolls. With a cry that seemed to rend heaven and earth, he called out, "*Shma Yisroel*–Hear, O Israel, the Lord is God, the Lord is One!"

With all his strength he cried out, "The Lord is God!" Seven times he said it, each time louder than the time before. The seventh time, he seemed to shout it with superhuman strength. As he said the word "God," his soul departed and returned to its Maker. The *poritz* was dead.

Reb Leib himself supervised the burial, which took place that same night. He made sure the *poritz* was buried in a Jewish cemetery. "Fortunate is one who dies with the name of God on his lips. He is a true *tzadik*," said Reb Leib at the funeral.

From that time on, Reb Leib said *kaddish* every Yom Kippur for the soul of the *poritz* who had become a true *baal teshuvah*.

REB MOSHE OF PRESHVORSK

Born:	?
Died:	1805 (5505)
Lived in:	Galicia
His *rebbe*:	Reb Elimelech of Lyzhansk
His successor:	*Chozeh* of Lublin, who studied under him
Best known as:	A hidden *tzadik*, whose greatness was revealed after his death when his writings were discovered

✳ 17 ✳

Oy, Oy, Ahhh, Ahhh

Reb Moshe of Preshvorsk used to go to the *mikvah* every day before praying. Rain, snow, sleet, or ice–nothing could prevent him from his daily immersion in the purifying waters. He would take his young son with him, too, to train him in this practice.

One winter morning, the *mikvah* waters were ice-cold. Shivering, Reb Moshe's son dipped one foot into the chilly water and yelled, "Oy! Oy!" He braced himself and immersed his whole body in the purifying waters.

When the boy came out, his body tingled with warmth. As he toweled himself dry, he sighed pleasurably, "Ahhh, ahhh."

Hearing him, his father smiled. "That is the difference between a *mitzvah* and an *aveirah*. When a person does a bad deed, first he says, "Ahhh," and afterward he cries out with regret, "Oy!" When he does a good deed, first he cries out, "Oy!" because it's hard, and afterward he sighs happily and says, "Ahhh."

REB LEVI YITZCHAK OF BERDICHEV

Born:	1740 (5500)
Died:	1809 (5570)
Lived in:	The Ukraine
His *rebbe*:	*Magid* of Mezhirech
Best known for:	His love of all Jews; author of *Kedushas Levi*

✳ 18 ✳

The Miser of Zhitomir

ot far from the home Reb Levi Yitzchak of Berdichev in the town of Zhitomir, there lived an old Jewish man named Yankel and his wife, Riva. They were as rich as they were stingy, never opening their hearts to the pleas of the needy. The rich man got richer by lending money at high interest to the Ukrainian peasants and farmers in the nearby villages. Yankel also demanded that the farmers supply him with eggs and cheese whenever they came to town. Riva ran her own business. She hoarded the money she earned in a secret place.

Yankel and Riva had an only son, Shmuel, who had a wife and six children. He eked out a bare living. Both parents and children often went hungry. But the stingy Yankel never once offered to help his son and his family.

One day Riva fell seriously ill. She lay in bed, too sick even to talk. Yankel was concerned about his wife, but he was more concerned about what she had done with her money.

"Where did you hide your money?" he begged her repeatedly to tell him. But she did not answer him. Perhaps she gave the money away to our son, he agonized. The thought upset him so much that he decided to go to Berdichev to seek the advice of Reb Levi Yitzchak, of saintly memory.

"My wife is sick and cannot tell me where her money is. She might have given it away. I am so worried. Please, *Rebbe*, pray for my wife, so she will get better," pleaded Yankel.

But the *rebbe* was not sympathetic. "If you do not change your ways, Yankel, troubles worse than this will befall you. Have pity on your son and your six starving grandchildren, and help them!"

The *rebbe*'s words cut to Yankel's heart. "I will change my ways and be a more generous person from now on," he resolved.

Upon his arrival home, business awaited Yankel. The *poritz* had sent a servant to deliver a letter to him. "I have heard that you make high-interest loans," the letter read. "I need two thousand rubles. Please lend it to me at whatever interest you name. I will be waiting for you to bring it."

"What a lucky windfall!" thought Yankel gleefully. While the servant waited, Yankel counted out two thousand rubles. He and the servant climbed into the carriage and set off for the *poritz*'s estate. The resolve Yankel had made to the *rav* was completely forgotten.

It was not destined for Yankel to ever get there. As the carriage passed through a lonely stretch of woods, a band of robbers swooped down upon them.

"Your money or your life!" they shouted. Brandishing an axe in front of the trembling old man, one of them yelled, "Hand over your money or we'll chop off your head!"

The terrified Yankel begged them to spare him. "Don't kill me! Have pity on me! I'm a poor man," he pleaded.

They might have believed him, but the *poritz*'s servant betrayed him. "He's lying," the servant told them. "He's very rich. He has two thousand rubles with him."

Furious at being lied to, the robbers fell to beating the unfortunate Yankel. "Master of the World," Yankel cried out desperately, "save me! I promise to give one thousand rubles to *tzedakah* if I get out of this alive."

Just then the sound of an approaching vehicle could be heard. It was the government mail carriage. "Let's get out of here!" the bandits cried. Letting Yankel go, they scattered in all directions.

Yankel waved weakly to the mailmen, who helped Yankel and the servant into their carriage and drove them back to Yankel's home. Yankel rejoiced to be alive. He was especially happy that he still had his two thousand rubles. The promise he had made to God about giving one thousand to *tzedakah* totally slipped his mind, and it was life as usual once again.

A few weeks later, Yankel was sitting in his rickety old house. He had never fixed it up because he could not bear to spend any money on it. Suddenly the walls and rafters of the room caved in and crashed down on top of him. His body was crushed by the great weight of the masonry.

With the remaining strength he had, the old man called out, "Help! Help!" as loudly as he could. Some neighbors heard his cries and came running. With great effort they succeeded in extricating him, more dead than alive, from beneath the toppled walls.

Doctors were summoned. Upon seeing his condition, they shook their heads doubtfully. "He won't pull through," they predicted.

Now both of them, the old man and his wife, who was still sick, lay in their beds with very little hope of recovery.

News of the accident reached their son. Shmuel came quickly to see his father. He was very distressed at his father's predicament, but a little part of him could not help but rejoice at the prospect of the ample inheritance awaiting him.

News also reached the ears of Yankel's brother Yehuda, who was a poor but kindhearted person. Though he, too, had never enjoyed any of his brother's large fortune, he felt deeply concerned about his brother. He decided to go to the Berdichever *rav* to ask him to pray for his brother's recovery.

Reb Levi Yitzchak's response took Yehuda by surprise. "I told him once before that he would suffer greatly if he did not abandon his uncaring, tightfisted ways, but he ignored my warning."

"Then there is nothing that can be done?" Yehuda asked anxiously.

"No, he still has a chance. He can still change," responded the *tzadik*. "If he stops being miserly and gives generously to those in need, I guarantee he will get better."

Yehuda rushed off to Zhitomir to report to his brother the words of the *rav*. The desire to live is great, and this time, Yankel heeded the *rav*'s warning. He entrusted Yehuda with the keys to his money box, saying, "I authorize you to give *tzedakah* generously to whomever you think deserves it."

The first thing Yehuda did was to give his nephew Shmuel several thousand rubles. The second thing he did was to repair the house so that it was safe and livable. After that, Yehuda opened the house for passersby, wayfarers, and poor people to stop in. He served them food and drink and gave them a place to rest. Before they left, he made sure to fill the pockets of the poor with rubles.

Just as the *tzadik* had predicted, the merit of the *tzedakah* had a beneficial result. One day followed another, and slowly but steadily, Yankel got stronger. Riva, his wife, also regained her health.

One day, Yankel felt strong enough to get up. The first thing he did was to examine the contents of his money box. So much was gone! "Yehuda, come quick!" he shouted.

Alarmed, Yehuda hurried to his brother's side. "What's the matter?" he asked worriedly.

"My money – it's all gone!"

"That's not true. You have plenty left. You're still a rich man," responded Yehuda.

"No, no," sobbed Yankel. "There was so much more. I can't believe how much you spent! How could you have done such a thing?"

"But you told me to," Yehuda tried to reason with him. "You told me to give *tzedakah* generously as the *rebbe* had said you should. I followed your instructions. Look, Yankel, you are healthy. Your wife is well now. Wasn't it worth it?"

"No, no," moaned Yankel. "I never meant for you to use up all this." He was breathing with difficulty, and his face was turning red. "I feel terrible," whispered Yankel, clutching at his heart. He looked as if he was about to collapse.

"Yankel," his brother entreated him, "why make yourself sick? Why regret all the good deeds your money did? Besides, there is plenty of money left!"

"You don't understand," groaned the sick man. "I worked so hard for that money, and now it's gone!" His face was purple.

Yehuda made no response, as it was obvious there was no reasoning with his brother. He was alarmed at his brother's state of health. His brother's face had turned a terrible color and his eyes were glazed. Yankel had evidently suffered a serious relapse.

The doctors were called once again. A brief examination revealed that the old man was in worse condition than ever before. This time the doctors were right. Yankel never recovered. In a few days he died.

Yankel's great wealth was inherited by his son, Shmuel. In gratitude to his uncle for all that he had done, Shmuel insisted that Yehuda and his wife come to live with him and his family, which they did.

Shmuel, unlike his father, knew how to use the gift of wealth wisely. He lived grandly in the manner of a wealthy man; he spent his days distributing abundant amounts of *tzedakah* and welcoming the poor into his home; he spent his nights studying Torah. His reputation as a generous philanthropist and *machnis orach* spread far and wide.

❈ 19 ❈

Olam Habo Guaranteed

ukkos was approaching, and in the town of Berdichev there were no *esrogim*. The holy Reb Levi Yitzchak paced up and down his room worriedly.

"What shall we do?" fretted the *tzadik*. "We *must* have an *esrog* for Sukkos!" He banged one fist into the palm of his other hand. "We must search until we find one. *Yogata umatzasa taamin* – if you work hard, you must surely succeed."

"Where shall we look?" the *talmidim* wondered. "We've already combed through all of Berdichev."

"Go out on the road outside the town," he bade them. "Who knows what you'll find there?"

The *talmidim* waited at the crossroads near the town. There they spied a Jew traveling homeward. They pounced on him. "Do you happen to have an *esrog* for Sukkos?"

"Yes, I do," he replied. "But it's not for sale. I need it for myself and my family."

"Please come with us to our *rav*," they beseeched him. "He wants to talk to you."

The traveler, whose name was Asher, could not very well refuse to talk to the well-known *tzadik* of Berdichev. So he went. The next thing he knew he was standing in the presence of the *tzadik*.

"*Shalom aleichem*, Reb Yid!" the Berdichever *rav* greeted him. "You have the opportunity of a lifetime now. If you agree, the whole Jewish population of Berdichev will be able to fulfill the *mitzvah* of *lulav* and *esrog* this Sukkos. Think of it! What a tremendous merit you will gain by staying here for the holiday!"

"*Rebbe*, I was on my way home for the *yom tov*. I want to spend Sukkos with my wife and children," replied Asher firmly.

"My friend, not only will you gain this great merit, but I'll bless you too. What are you lacking? I will bless you with children. Or do you need a blessing for *parnosoh*?"

Asher would not budge. "I don't need anything. My wife and I have a nice family and I make a decent living. Please permit me to continue on my way."

Reb Levi Yitzchak did not give up. "I promise you that you'll have a place with me in *olam habo*."

This was an offer Asher could not turn down. After all, who knew better than he how many sins and wrongdoings he had committed in his life? Who knew how many opportunities he had missed to do good deeds? And now he would have nothing more to worry about, for a *tzadik*—and none less than the Berdichever *tzadik*—was guaranteeing him a place in the world to come.

Asher gave in. "It's a deal," he said. "I'll stay."

It was the first night of Sukkos. The evening prayers over, everyone hurried out of the *shul*. No one seemed to notice Asher. The *shul* had emptied out. He was the only one left. Asher's feelings were hurt. "Here they beg me to stay in their town for *yom tov* and then they don't even invite me!" he mulled. "Well, maybe they just forgot." He swallowed his pride and approached the first *sukkah* he saw. "*Gut yom tov!*" he called out. "Would you like a guest for the *yom tov* meal?"

When they saw who it was, they shook their heads. "We don't have any room. Sorry."

Asher's face turned red from embarrassment and disappointment. Was this a way to treat a visitor? What inhospitable people the people of Berdichev were! He tried a second *sukkah*. "It's Asher," he introduced himself. "Reb Levi Yitzchak asked me to spend the *yom tov* in your town so all of you could *bentsh* on my *esrog*."

"I'm sorry, we can't accommodate you," was the response.

"I'll bring my own food. I just need a place to sit in the *sukkah*," he pleaded.

"We can't help you." They remained adamant.

What should he do? Where should he go? He *must* eat in a *sukkah* tonight. It was Sukkos and that was the *mitzvah* of Sukkos—to eat in the *sukkah*. He approached yet a third family's *sukkah*. They too refused to let him in. "Why?" he exploded. "Why won't you let me in? I insist that you tell me!"

"Because," came the shocking reply, "the *rav* told us not to."

Asher could not believe his ears. The *rav* had told them not to? Was this the reward he got for doing the *rav* a favor? He rushed over in a rage to the home of Reb Levi Yitzchak.

"*Gut yom tov*," the *rav* calmly greeted him.

"*Gut yom tov?*" screeched Asher. "How can I have a *gut yom tov* when you forbade everyone to let me into their *sukkos*? What kind of repayment is this for the favor I did for you and for the inconvenience I suffer for being here?"

"How important is it for you to eat in a *sukkah* tonight?" the *tzadik* inquired.

"What do you mean 'how important'? It's very important!" Asher was indignant.

"Would you be willing to release me of my promise to you about your share in the world to come?" asked the *rav*.

Asher stepped back in stunned surprise. Give up the rabbi's promise so that he could eat in the *sukkah*? Why, even if he *didn't* eat in a *sukkah*, he had a place guaranteed in *olam habo*. For that matter, even if he never did another *mitzvah* in his whole life, he had that place guaranteed.

On the other hand, Asher thought, it would mean he wouldn't eat in a *sukkah* on Sukkos. He would have to give up the precious *mitzvah*. How could he do that? He just could not bring himself to eat in a house, as if it were a regular day.

"You win," he sighed resignedly.

"No," answered the *tzadik* quietly. "*You* win. I was testing you to see how dear the *mitzvah* was to you. You showed me now that you are willing to give up your guaranteed place in *olam habo* in order to eat in a *sukkah*. Now I know that you truly deserve the reward I promised you. You have my word once again that it is yours."

Tears of joy, relief, and gratitude welled up in Asher's eyes.

Reb Levi Yitzchak gave orders to the people of Berdichev to invite Asher into their *sukkos* and to treat him with the utmost respect. Suddenly everyone was fighting over him. Everyone wanted the honor of having him as their guest.

※ **20** ※

The Secret Side of Reb Nasan, the Miser

There wasn't much the people of Berdichev knew about Reb Nasan. Only two things were known to everyone: Reb Nasan was rich and he was a miser. So when his time in this world was up and Reb Nasan died, most people were not too sorry.

Reb Nasan's family went to the *Chevrah Kadisha* to buy a burial plot for him. To their surprise, the *Chevrah Kadisha* demanded a very high fee for the plot.

"Why are you charging us more than you charge anyone else?" they protested angrily. "It's not fair!"

"Well, your father never helped out in the community when he was alive. At least we'll get some money out of him now," they retorted.

"You have no right to do that!" they shouted.

The bickering and arguing continued. Neither side would give in. "Let's ask the Berdichever *rav* to settle our disagreement," suggested the *Chevrah Kadisha* finally.

So the family of the deceased and the *Chevrah Kadisha* presented their cases before the holy Reb Levi Yitzchak of Berdichev. They waited to hear the *rav's* verdict.

"Reb Nasan's family is right. They should not be forced to pay an unreasonable sum of money to bury the deceased," ruled the *tzadik* to the chagrin of the *Chevrah Kadisha*. "I am deeply grieved to hear of the passing of Reb Nasan, however," he added sadly. "I would like to be at his *levayah*. Please let me know when the funeral will take place."

Why was the *rav* so saddened by the man's death? Hadn't Reb Nasan been a stingy miser? Why was the *rav* going to the funeral? Could Reb Nasan have been a special man after all? Everyone was puzzled. Yet, when they heard that the Berdichever *rav* was accompanying the deceased to his grave, people stopped what they were doing and joined the *levayah*— not so much out of respect for Reb Nasan as out of respect for the *tzadik*. So in the end, Reb Nasan was accompanied in his final journey to his eternal resting place by the whole town of Berdichev.

After the funeral was over, one brave *talmid* ventured to ask the *rav*, "Was there something about Reb Nasan that we didn't know? Everyone thought that he was a tightfisted miser. Were we wrong?"

"Reb Nasan was a *tzadik* and gave *tzedakah* generously. Only he did his good deeds secretly. I myself didn't know about them until I had three cases brought before me in which Reb Nasan was involved. Let me tell you what they were, and you can judge for yourself."

Case 1 – The Regretful Money-Finder

A traveling Jewish merchant once came to do business in a certain city. He was transacting some business when he reached into his pocket and found his money was gone. A cry of dismay escaped his lips. He had lost a huge amount of money. The world grew black before his eyes. He fainted.

"Get a doctor!" someone called. A crowd quickly gathered around the unconscious man.

A doctor was rushed to the scene. The doctor revived the businessman from his faint. As consciousness returned to him, he remembered his great loss. "My money," he murmured. "It's gone!" And he fell back into a faint.

Once more the doctor revived him. But again the merchant blacked out when he recalled his loss. This happened again and again until the doctor raised his hands in despair and declared, "It's no use. He'll just keep fainting unless he gets his money back."

Suddenly a stranger was seen pushing his way through the crowd. "I found the missing money! How much was it that was lost?" he called out.

The merchant, who was in between faints, heard. He told the stranger—it was Reb Nasan—how much he had lost.

"There, I have it!" declared Reb Nasan. He handed the money to the businessman, who gratefully accepted it.

Soon the businessman was breathing normally again, and the color returned to his formerly pale face. After a couple of hours he felt stronger and soon was well enough to continue on his business travels to the next town.

A few days later, two people appeared before Reb Levi Yitzchak asking him to settle a dispute. The first party was a stranger to Reb Levi Yitzchak. He came from the same city where the businessman had lost his money.

The second party was Reb Nasan.

The stranger spoke first. "*I* was the one who found the lost money, not Reb Nasan."

"So why didn't you give it back right away?" asked the Berdichever *rav*.

"Well, I kept it at first, but now my conscience bothers me," replied the stranger. "So I want to pay Reb Nasan back now. But he won't take the money."

It was Reb Nasan's turn to speak now. "I gave that merchant the money because it was a question of life and death. If I accept the money from you now, that means I am giving up the merit of having saved the life of another Jew, and I'm not willing to do that!"

The *rav* pondered the case for a few minutes before rendering his decision. "Reb Nasan is right. If Reb Nasan does not want to be repaid, his wish must be respected. As for you," the *rav* addressed the stranger, "I know you feel bad about what you did, but you'll have to find another way to make up for it."

That case gave the Berdichever *rav* his first glimpse into the true character of Reb Nasan.

Then came the next *Din Torah*.

Case 2 – The Thursday Pick-ups

There lived in Berdichev a man by the name of Simcha, who, try as he might, could not make ends meet. One day he proposed to his wife, Chaya, the following idea: "I would like to try my fortune in another country. Maybe I'll succeed there and bring you back a lot of money. Won't that be nice?"

His wife refused to hear of it. "How will I manage without you? And what will the children do without a father? And besides, how will we survive financially while you are away?"

The husband persisted, but his wife held firm. One day Simcha said to her, "I have arranged for all your needs while I will be away making my fortune. I made an agreement with a wealthy man in this city. His accountant will give you money every Thursday for you and the children to live on."

Reluctantly Chaya gave in. Simcha packed up his things and bade his family good-bye. Tearfully Chaya and the children waved to him. When would they see him again? Would he really succeed? Would she and the children manage without him? Chaya asked herself these questions as she watched her husband depart.

The next Thursday, Chaya went to the address her husband had given her. "I'm here to pick up my money," she informed the accountant at the desk.

"What money?" asked the puzzled accountant.

"You're supposed to give me money every Thursday. That's what my husband, Simcha, arranged with you before he left," Chaya replied.

"I don't know you. I never saw you before. And I never heard of your husband Simcha. I don't know about any agreement like that. You must have come to the wrong place." And the accountant got up to show her to the door.

"I didn't make any mistake! Look! Here is the name and address my husband left me. You're trying to cheat me out of my rightful money!" Chaya's voice rose in panic and anger.

The accountant shouted, "Lady, you're crazy! Get out of here!"

The screams and shouts soon reached the ears of the accountant's employer. The door opened and in he walked. It was Reb Nasan.

"What's all the hollering about?" he demanded to know.

"My husband, Simcha, made an agreement with you before he left Berdichev that as long as he was out of the country you would take care of my family's needs. And now," Chaya pointed accusingly at the accountant, "he denies that any agreement was made. He's trying to rob me of my money!"

"Oh, yes!" the employer exclaimed, clapping his hand to his forehead as if he had just remembered something. "I was so busy that I forgot to mention it to my accountant. Please forgive him. Here's your money. And be sure to come back every Thursday, and we'll have the money ready for you."

Chaya heaved a sigh of relief as she stuffed the money into her purse.

From then on, she showed up each Thursday at the rich man's office, where she was given her weekly stipend. With the money she was able to feed herself and the children during the many weeks and months that her husband was away.

At long last, Simcha returned. He had succeeded very well after all and had acquired a considerable fortune.

"And how," Simcha cleared his throat nervously, "how did you manage, uh, financially, while I was gone?"

"No problem. I did exactly what you told me to. Every Thursday I picked up the money from Reb Nasan's accountant. The first time I went I had a little trouble, but after that it was fine."

"Is that so?" Simcha's eyes opened wide with amazement.

At the first opportunity, Simcha hastened to the home of Reb Nasan. "I am very thankful to you for having supported my wife and children while I was gone, and I'm sorry if I caused you any trouble. I would like to repay you now," said Simcha.

"I have no business with you," replied the wealthy man coolly. "I don't even know you."

"You helped my wife out, and I would like to pay you back.

So please take the money," Simcha said, trying to push the money into Reb Nasan's hand.

Reb Nasan remained firm. "I helped your wife and children because I wanted to. I made no agreement with you," he replied.

"Then let's go to a *Din Torah*," Simcha insisted. "Let the *rav* decide."

So the two of them came to Reb Levi Yitzchak and presented their cases to him.

"Reb Nasan is right. He gave the money from his own free will. He cannot be compelled to accept any return for it" was the *rav*'s verdict.

Reb Nasan went away contented. No one could take away his *mitzvah* of having supported a poor Jewish woman and her children when they needed it.

Case 3 – God, the Cosigner

At the home of the wealthy Reb Nasan, there once arrived a stranger with a request. "I had a thriving business here in Berdichev," the man, whose name was Daniel, told Reb Nasan, "but the business failed. If I could only have a nice-sized loan, then I would be able to get back on my feet once more, with God's help. Would it be possible for you to lend me the money, and I'll pay you back as soon as my business does well?"

"Who will cosign your loan?" inquired the rich man, for that is how most loans are made. Another person promises that if the borrower cannot pay back the money, that person will pay it back. That person is called the cosigner.

"I don't have anybody to be my cosigner," sighed the poor

businessman. Just then an idea flashed into Daniel's head. "God will be my cosigner!" he declared.

"That's good enough for me," responded Reb Nasan smilingly. The two of them set a date by which time the loan would be repaid, and Reb Nasan lent Daniel the money he had asked for.

When the day arrived by which the loan was supposed to be repaid, there was no sign of Daniel. More time passed, and still there was no word from the borrower. One day Daniel appeared. "I apologize for being late with the money," he said, "but I have it now."

"That's okay," answered Reb Nasan. "It's not necessary to pay me back."

The businessman was astounded. "What do you mean? I borrowed money from you, and I want to repay it. I'm truly sorry I'm late, but the business didn't pick up as fast as I had hoped. Please accept the money now."

"I was paid back already," Reb Nasan assured him. "I don't need to be repaid twice."

"You were paid back?" Daniel was perplexed. "How could that be?"

"Your cosigner repaid me," was the response of Reb Nasan.

"My cosigner, my cosigner," muttered Daniel, trying to recall who the cosigner on the loan was. He suddenly remembered. "Why, God was my cosigner!"

"That's exactly right. I have done very well since I made you the loan, and I consider that God's repayment to me," said Reb Nasan with a tone of finality.

Daniel persisted, however. "If you won't take back the money, I'll take you to a *Din Torah*," he threatened.

"That's fine with me," shrugged the wealthy man.

So, for the third time, Reb Nasan appeared as a litigant before the *rav* of Berdichev.

And, for the third time, Reb Levi Yitzchak ruled in favor of Reb Nasan, the so-called miser.

"So you see, my friends," concluded the *rav*, "although the whole world thought Reb Nasan was a stingy miser, the truth was that he was a very kind and giving person. But when he helped people, he didn't want anybody to know about it. Reb Nasan performed the very highest form of *tzedakah*—charity given in secret."

✳ 21 ✳

The Troublemaker

he *rebbe* Reb Baruch of Medzhibozh, grandson of the Baal Shem Tov, was once staying at an inn with his *talmidim*. Suddenly they heard a knock at the door. It was Reb Levi Yitzchak of Berdichev.

"Uh-oh," groaned Reb Baruch. "He's going to make trouble. I know him. Please don't let him in."

But Reb Levi Yitzchak did not go away.

Peeking through the window, the Jewish innkeeper saw Reb Levi Yitzchak and protested, "Why, he looks like an honorable rabbi. Can't I let him in?"

Reb Baruch relented. "Okay, let him in," he said with a sigh, "but only on one condition. Only if he agrees to be quiet and not make any trouble."

Reb Levi Yitzchak had no choice. He agreed to the condition, and the innkeeper brought him in.

At suppertime, all the guests gathered in the dining room — Reb Baruch, his disciples, Reb Levi Yitzchak, and the other guests. The innkeeper served his guests, going from one table to the other.

He came to the table of the Berdichever *rav* with a pepper grinder in hand. "Don't you love pepper?" the innkeeper asked the *rav*, smacking his lips.

The *rav* became very upset. "Do I love pepper?" he asked indignantly. He jumped up onto the bench and shrieked, "DO I LOVE PEPPER? IT'S GOD I LOVE, NOT PEPPER!" And he remained in a frenzy for a long time, jumping and rolling over and shouting, "DO I LOVE PEPPER?" until the innkeeper and the other guests didn't know what to do.

Said Reb Baruch with a twinkle in his eye, "See what I mean? Reb Levi Yitzchak makes trouble wherever he goes."

❋❋ 22 ❋❋

The Forty-eight-Hour Yom Kippur

The author of the *Yeshuos Yaakov*, though a respected scholar, did not approve of *chasidim* and their ways. But one Yom Kippur he had a chance to observe Reb Levi Yitzchak of Berdichev, and he was forced had to admit he had been wrong.

It happened like this. The Berdichever *rav* arrived in Lvov, where Reb Yaakov lived. He was invited by a wealthy, upstanding member of the community to stay in his home. Reb Levi Yitzchak's host, a rich man, quickly realized that his guest was a saintly, learned man, and he sent a message to the other heads of the community. "We have here visiting in our city a very holy man. Shall we ask him to be our *baal tefillah* [*chazan*] on Yom Kippur?"

"By all means," the community heads agreed.

On *erev* Yom Kippur, they sent the town *shammes* to Reb Levi Yitzchak. The *shammes*, however, returned alone. "I don't think he'll make an appropriate *chazan* for us," sniffed the *shammes*. "He's sitting around, talking with friends, and drinking mead. He's really not behaving in the proper *erev* Yom Kippur spirit."

They debated among themselves for a while. "Call him anyway," they decided.

So the *shammes* requested the *rav* from Berdichev to be the *baal tefillah*, and the *rav* consented.

He approached the *bimah* and, with a great cry bursting from his lips, began the *Kol Nidrei*. The congregants trembled with awe to hear him. He led the rest of the evening prayers the same way—powerfully, emotionally, tearfully. At the end of the service, he sang *Adon Olam* with ardor.

Most of the people went home to sleep that night. A few remained to study Torah or recite *tehillim*, the Yeshuos Yaakov among them. He could not help noticing Reb Levi Yitzchak.

The Berdichever *rav* had taken out the tractate *Yoma*. He opened it to page one. Reb Yaakov watched and listened as the *rav* began to study. He delved into the Talmud in such depth that the author of the *Yeshuos Yaakov*, a learned man himself, was astounded. "He studies like the old great scholars," he muttered to himself.

Soon Reb Yaakov grew tired and went home to sleep. In the morning, when he returned to *shul*, he was curious to see what Reb Levi Yitzchak was doing. To Reb Yaakov's amazement, the *rav* was on the last page of *Yoma*. He had been up all night studying the tractate. The Yeshuos Yaakov answered *amen* as the *rav* made the traditional *siyum* — completion ceremony — over the finished tractate.

Again Reb Levi Yitzchak was *baal tefillah*. Though he hadn't slept a wink, though he was fasting, though he wasn't a young man anymore, the *rav* prayed with great zeal. All day long his strength did not diminish. He prayed, sang, and read the Torah, all with the same fiery ador.

When Yom Kippur was over, the *rav* returned to the home of his host, who had prepared a variety of tempting foods for his distinguished guest to break his fast on.

"I must have my nourishment," the *rav* declared. The host naturally assumed that Reb Levi Yitzchak was referring to some tasty snack that he had brought along. How surprised he was to see the *shammes* bringing the *rav* a *Gemora*!

"Ahhhh," murmured the *rav* as he opened the tractate *Sukkah*. "Now I feel better." All night long and all through the next day, the Berdichever *rav* immersed himself in the *Gemora* in preparation for the upcoming festival of Sukkos.

That night the *rav* finally broke his fast. It had been forty-eight hours since he had eaten or drunk anything.

After seeing how the Berdichever *rav* spent his Yom Kippur, the author of the *Yeshuos Yaakov* developed new respect for *chasidim*.

REB YISROEL OF KOZNITZ

Born: 1740 (5500)
Died: 1814 (5575)
Lived in: Poland
His *rebbes*: *Magid* of Mezhirech, Reb Shmelke of Nikolsburg, Reb Elimelech of Lyzhansk
His successor: His son Reb Moshe Eliakim of Koznitz
Best known for: Intensity of prayer despite his physical weakness
Also called: Koznitzer *Magid*

✸ 23 ✸

A *Gut* Purim

ershon was poor—no, not poor—destitute. His children were gaunt with hunger. He worried about them constantly. Where would he get money to pay for a piece of black bread or a bowl of borscht for his family?

When Purim came, Gershon left his village and trekked to Koznitz. It was Purim, after all, and he had to hear the *Megillah*. He came to the *beis midrash* of the holy Koznitzer *Magid* and listened to the *Magid* read the *Megillah*.

The morning *Shachris* prayers over, Gershon prepared to return home. How surprised he was to hear the *Magid* address him! "Reb Yid," the *Magid* called to him. "Aren't you from the neighboring village? How is it you didn't bring me *shalach monos*?"

The villager's head whirled. Why, he hadn't even thought of it, if truth be told. It was the custom for the congregation to bring their rabbi *shalach monos* on Purim. But how could he? He didn't have money even to feed his own starving family, let alone buy food for *shalach monos*.

The *rebbe* saw his confusion. "Come, my friend. Let us make a *l'chaim*. It's Purim today!"

Gershon joined the *Magid* and his *chasidim* in the *Magid*'s home. There he ate honey cake and gulped down a few *l'chaims* of whiskey. Around him people were happy. They sang songs and made merry. Gershon too caught the spirit of Purim. A new feeling of confidence and gladness overwhelmed him.

"The *rebbe* wants me to give him *shalach monos*," he said to himself. "I must find a way. I *will* find a way." He went to the wine merchant. "A *gut* Purim!" he greeted the shopkeeper spiritedly.

"A *gut* Purim," the wine merchant returned, though a trifle more quietly.

"Give me please a bottle of fine wine," requested Gershon. "I can't pay you today, but I'll pay you some other time. And if not—why, it's Purim today, isn't it?"

Gershon's exuberance was infectious. "Certainly," the surprised wine merchant responded, handing Gershon a bottle of sparkling red wine.

Next Gershon went to the grocer. "A *gut* Purim!" he cried out merrily.

The grocer chuckled at Gershon's enthusiasm. Here was someone who knew what Purim joy was. "A *gut* Purim to you!" he replied.

"May I have some of your best apples? I'll pay you another time. And if not, it's Purim after all!" exclaimed the villager.

"Why, of course!" exclaimed the grocer.

Gershon put together his wine and apples and sprinted back to the Koznitzer *Magid*. "I brought the *rebbe shalach monos*," he announced.

The *rebbe* accepted it graciously. "You did a good thing, Reb Yid. I want you to remember to bring me *shalach monos* on Purim every year."

Satisfied that he had done the *rebbe*'s bidding, the villager realized that actually it hadn't been so hard after all. Maybe he could do the same for his own family. How delighted they would all be to have something in their stomachs. Their Purim would indeed be a happy one.

"A *gut* Purim!" he declared to the bartender. "May I have some vodka on credit? And if I don't pay, it's Purim after all." The bartender gave him vodka.

Gershon went to the baker and got some bread in the same way. Then he got some salted herring. To everyone he loudly called *"Gut* Purim!"

He hurried back to his village, imagining how excited his wife and children would be when he got home with his package. He opened the door and called out happily, "It's Purim today! A *gut* Purim, everyone!"

His wife and children eyed him suspiciously. They had never seen him in such a boisterous mood before. Had he gone crazy, God forbid?

He placed the bread, the fish, and the liquor on the table. "Eat and drink to your hearts' content. It's Purim after all, isn't it?"

The children ran to the table and joyfully began eating. He and his wife joined them. They drank a couple of vodkas, and soon everyone was happily wishing each other "a *gut* Purim!" They danced around the table and sang joyfully. As the villager and his family were celebrating the Purim *seudah*, they heard a knock at the door.

"Don't open it, my dear," said Gershon to his wife. "It's probably one of the peasants coming to disrupt our celebration."

The knocking wouldn't stop, however.

"It might be the man who brings us potatoes," Gershon's

wife suggested. "I'd better open up for him." She opened up the door, and a Polish farmer, more dead than alive, fell in. He was completely covered with terrible wounds. Gershon and his wife washed off his wounds. They gave the unfortunate man vodka to revive his spirits and bread to eat.

After the stranger had eaten and drunk, he felt a little better. "Thank you for taking care of me," he murmured.

"Who did that to you?" they asked horrified, pointing to the bruises and wounds all over his body.

"My son beat me—my own son," he answered bitterly. "I thought he would kill me. But he's not going to get the money I hid. Not after what he did to me. I will give it to you instead because you were kind to me." The farmer took Gershon to the woods and showed him where he had hidden a chestful of money under a tree. He never recovered totally, and died soon after. Gershon and his wife dug up the hidden treasure. There was a huge number of gold coins. They would never have to worry about money the rest of their lives.

And every year on Purim, Gershon made a joyous celebration. Most important, he never forgot to send the Koznitzer *Magid* a very generous package of *shalach monos*.

REB MOSHE LEIB
OF SASOV

Born: 1745 (5505)
Died: 1807 (5567
Lived in: Galicia
His *rebbe*: Reb Shmelka of Nikolsburg
Best known for: His devotion to and love of the Jews

✳ 24 ✳

Reb Yudel Is Foiled

Reb Yudel Nathanson of the city of Brody did not like *chasidim* or their *rebbe*. He could not stand it when *chasidim* praised their *rebbe* Reb Moshe Yehuda Leib Sasover. *Chasidim* told Reb Yudel, "Our *rebbe* always says hello first to everyone. Whenever he meets someone, he's always the first one to say *shalom aleichem*." When he heard that, Reb Yudel would gnash his teeth in rage. He thought, how could it be that the Sasover *always* said hello first and that there *never* was a time that someone said hello first to him? Surely there had to be times when someone else said hello first to the *rebbe*!

And then he heard statements such as "At the stroke of midnight our *rebbe*, Reb Moshe Yehuda Leib Sasover, always wakes up to say *Tikun Chatzos*." Did their *rebbe always* wake up at exactly twelve o'clock in the night to say the midnight prayer? Didn't he *ever* oversleep? Reb Yudel Nathanson found it very hard to believe that every single night at the exact hour of midnight , the Sasover *rebbe* always got up without fail.

"I'm sick and tired of hearing about their 'holy' *rebbe*. I'll show those *chasidim*, once and for all, that their boasts about their *rebbe* are false," Reb Yudel decided.

Soon his opportunity came. Reb Yudel heard that Reb Moshe Yehuda Leib Sasover had come to Brody. Reb Yudel hired two men. "I want to show the world that all those things they say about the Sasover *rebbe* are not true," he told them secretly. "I want you to go and say hello to him first, before he has a chance to say it to you. Then the *chasidim* will see that he's not the great holy *tzadik* they think he is."

They went to the *mikvah*, knowing that the *tzadik* always immersed himself in the *mikvah* before prayer. They waited until the *tzadik* emerged. They tiptoed behind him silently, hardly breathing. Closer and closer they got. They were just about to sneak up on him, when suddenly the *rebbe* spun around and exclaimed, *"Gut Shabbos!"* The *tzadik* had beaten them to it.

Foiled! They clenched their fists in frustration!

Naturally, Reb Yudel was quite disappointed at their failure, but he did not give up. "This time I will do the job myself. That way I'll be sure the job gets done properly."

Reb Yudel sent a message to the *tzadik*. "I would be honored if you came to my home this evening."

Said Reb Moshe Yehuda Leib Sasover, "Reb Yudel, I hear, is something of a scholar. He's from a fine family and is a wealthy and upstanding member of the community. Tell him I'll be there tonight, after *Maariv*."

Reb Yudel greeted his guest cordially. "Come in! Come in!" he cried. "What an honored guest we have here!"

He ushered the *rebbe* into the dining room. The servants brought in platters of food and pitchers of beverages as befits a rich host. "Before I forget," said Reb Yudel, "I have heard you are active in the cause of *pidyon shvuyim*—redeeming Jewish prisoners and hostages. I would like to give you a donation for that." The *rebbe* acknowledged his host's generosity. "For such a revered guest as yourself I have something very special." Reb Yudel took out a bottle of sparkling red wine. "This is the best wine I could get. It is fit for kings and queens. I am sure you will like it. Please let me pour you some."

The *tzadik* caught the scent of the wine. It was heady, powerful stuff. "So this is what Reb Yudel is up to," Reb Moshe Leib thought. "He wants to put me into a deep sleep so that I should miss *Tikun Chatzos*."

It was ten o'clock. In two hours it would be time to say the midnight prayers. But Reb Moshe Leib had no choice. A good guest does what his host asks of him. He drank the wine. Soon his body tingled with warmth and his head began to spin. He fell into a deep sleep. The wine had done its work.

"My trick worked!" Reb Yudel was ecstatic. "He'll never wake up at midnight now. I'll show all those *chasidim* that they were wrong about their *rebbe*."

The *tzadik* slept on. Two hours crept by. Reb Yudel smiled with satisfaction. All at once his smile faded. The clock was striking midnight, and before his very eyes Reb Moshe Leib stirred. How could it be? It wasn't humanly possible! The *tzadik* had awoken! Reb Moshe Leib, completely sober, washed his hands and tearfully recited the prayer over the destruction of the Temple and the exile of the *Shechinah*.

"I give up! I give up!" Reb Yudel wrung his hands in frustration. "I admit he is a holy man after all!"

REB SHNEUR ZALMAN OF LYADY

Born:	1745 (5505)
Died:	1813 (5573)
Lived in:	White Russia
His *rebbe*:	*Magid* of Mezhirech
His successor:	His son Reb Dov Ber of Lubavitch
Best known as:	Founder of intellectual branch of *Chasidus* known as *Chabad*; author of the *Tanya* and *Shulchan Aruch HaRav*
Also called:	*Alter Rebbe*; the Baal HaTanya (for his book)

✸✸ 25 ✸✸

The Special Room

Two Jewish merchants once left the Russian Pale to go to trade deep in Russia where no Jews lived. There they lived for several years doing business with non-Jews. Little by little they abandoned their Jewish ways and adopted the ways of the Russian Gentiles.

After several years the merchants decided to go home. They had to travel a long distance. In the district of Kursk, in a village called Petyana, they entered an inn run by a sturdy old Russian.

"May we have some hot tea?" they inquired. The landlord poured them hot tea from the samovar. "We're very hungry," they said. "Can we have a hot, cooked meal?"

The landlord replied, "I'm sorry. I have no kosher meat."

The merchants laughed. "Whatever you have is fine for us," they told him.

"Well, you'll have to wait awhile. I need to heat up the oven first before I cook the meat," said the innkeeper.

"That's okay," the travelers answered. "We'll wait."

They sat and waited. Suddenly the landlord came back in. The men jumped in fright when they saw him. His face was red and angry. In his hand he brandished a wicked-looking axe.

"Get ready to die!" he exclaimed.

They turned pale with terror. "Why? What did we do? We're good people! We work hard for a living. Why do you want to kill us?" they pleaded.

"Because that's what I do. I rob travelers and then kill them," he snarled. The landlord locked them up in a room. The merchants could hear him sharpening his axe and saying to his son, "As soon as the sun comes up, I'm going to kill those Jews." Perhaps there was a way to escape, they thought desperately. They searched the whole room but could not find any.

"Why did we have to leave our hometown and come to these forsaken places?" they asked each other despairingly. "This would never have happened to us if we had remained in the Jewish Pale of Settlement."

The landlord came in again. "If you want to say your prayers before you die, I have a special room for that. Come this way."

The innkeeper led them to the special room. "Say your prayers because soon I will finish you both off," he threatened them.

As the two Jews entered the special room, they were over-come with such regret for the life-style they had led that they began sobbing bitterly. They wanted to pray and ask God for forgiveness, but it had been so many years since they had prayed that they could barely remember what to say. Slowly the words came back to them. *"Shma Yisroel*—Hear, O Israel, the Lord is our God, the Lord is One. God, please forgive us, for we have sinned," they prayed.

The door opened. There stood the landlord smiling. His axe was gone. The travelers' jaws dropped open in surprise. "Don't worry. I never really meant to hurt you," he assured them. "I just wanted to scare you."

"But why?" they asked, incredulous.

"Many years ago," the landlord explained, "a holy rabbi came to Petyana and stayed here. He became ill and passed away right here in this room. But before he died, he said to me that if any Jews should come here and ask for nonkosher food, I should pretend that I would kill them in order to get them to repent. Then he passed away. I never used this room again except when Jewish people came here and wanted to pray. When you came here and asked for nonkosher food, I remembered the holy sage's instructions. I pretended I was going to kill you. I brought you into this room so you should feel its holiness and be able to repent."

Who was the holy rabbi? They found out that it was the *Alter Rebbe*, Reb Shneur Zalman of Lyady. They went to his grave in Haiditz, and there they resumed their prayers of *teshuvah*, becoming devout God-fearing Jews.

✳ 26 ✳

The Arrest and Release of the
Alter Rebbe

Part 1
Disaster Strikes

On Rosh Hashanah of 1798, the *chasidim* noticed a hint of sadness in their *rebbe*'s voice. They could hear it in his prayers and in his reading of the Torah. They could see it in his dancing of the *hakafos* on Simchas Torah. When they saw the *Alter Rebbe* sad, they too became sad. They knew that something terrible was going to happen. With dread in their hearts, they waited to see what it would be.

Then it happened. The night after Simchas Torah, armed messengers from the czar appeared in Liozno. Banging on the door of the *Alter Rebbe*'s home, they shouted, "Open up in the name of the czar!"

The *rebbe* heard them and slipped out through a back door. He hid outside until they left. The czar's officers rode off, disappointed not to have found the man they were looking for. But Reb Shneur Zalman knew that they would be back.

He went to his friend Reb Shmuel Menkes, a devout *chasid*. "I need your advice," the *rebbe* said to him. "I know those officers will be back to arrest me. What should I do—hide again or give myself up?"

"I think you should give yourself up," advised Reb Shmuel.

Two days later the officers were back. "We're here to arrest Shneur Zalman!" they loudly announced. They entered the house and seized the *rebbe*. They led him to a coach that was used for the most dangerous criminals—those who had rebelled against the Czar. The coach was frightening to look at—all black and covered with iron bars. Everyone knew that those taken away in the black coach were never seen alive again.

The family, friends, and *chasidim* of the *rebbe* wept bitterly at seeing him depart. Where was he being taken? The guards would not tell them. Would they ever see their *rebbe* again? They did not know. Terror filled their hearts.

The *rebbe* was arrested on a Thursday night. The next day—Friday—at noon, the *rebbe* spoke to the guards. "*Shabbos* is coming, and I do not want to desecrate the holy *Shabbos*," he said. "Can you please stop the wagon?"

"Since when does a prisoner tell his guards what to do?" snorted the guards disdainfully. They ignored the *rebbe's* request.

Just then the axle of the wagon broke. The guards dismounted from the wagon and went to work fixing it. Then they climbed back into the wagon and told the driver to proceed.

The driver yelled, "Giddyap!" He struck the horse on his back with his whip. To his amazement one of the horses crumpled up and fell down.

The guards again dismounted to look at the fallen horse.

"He's dead!" exclaimed the guard.

"Well, get a new horse then!" ordered the officer in charge.

A fresh horse was brought and hitched to the wagon. The driver whipped the horses. The horses leaped up. They strained and pulled, but the coach would not budge. The officer whipped the horses harder and harder, but the horses could not move the wagon even one inch.

The officer threw up his hands in defeat. "I give up," he muttered to himself. "This prisoner is no ordinary man. Heaven seems to obey his wishes." He addressed the *rebbe* with new respect. "Would you allow us to ride just till the next village? Then we'll stop there till the *Shabbos* is over."

The *rebbe* refused.

The officer asked, "Then may we just move the coach to the side of the road?"

"You may," replied the *rebbe*.

The driver told the horses to go. The horses easily pulled the wagon over to the side of the road. The coach and its passengers remained there until the *Shabbos* was over. Then the coach resumed its journey.

Years later, a *chasid* passed by the place where the wagon

had rested that *Shabbos* long ago. He was very surprised at what he saw. As far as the eye could see, only short, stunted trees grew in the area. But in one spot – the spot where the *rebbe* had spent the *Shabbos* – there grew one majestic, tall tree, its branches spreading out toward the heavens.

The very same night that the *Alter Rebbe* was arrested, the *chasidim* called an emergency meeting. At the meeting, a committee was appointed. Its goal: to get the *rebbe* out of jail. Until that happened, the committee members were not to go to their jobs or do anything else except work at getting the *rebbe* freed.

The first thing they did was to make the following decisions for everyone to obey as long as the *rebbe* was in jail:

1. All men must fast every Monday and Thursday.
2. All week long only bread and water could be eaten. On *Shabbos*, one cooked dish could be eaten.
3. No weddings or engagements could take place. If a wedding was already scheduled it might take place, but no music could be played and no meat could be eaten.
4. The teachers should tell their students about the suffering of the *rebbe* in prison. They should recite the Psalms with their pupils.
5. Everyone should have money and jewelry ready in case the *rebbe* had to be ransomed or for any other expense that might occur in the effort to save the *rebbe*.
6. If, God forbid, anyone should pass away in that time, his *neshamah* would be sworn to inform the Baal Shem Tov and the *Magid* up in heaven that the *Alter Rebbe* was imprisoned and the *Torah* of *Chasidus* was in jeopardy.

The *chasidim* uncomplainingly accepted these decisions. They wanted with all their heart to have their *rebbe* back, safe and sound. They were willing and eager to undergo any sacrifice or fulfill any demands placed on them.

Right before the *Alter Rebbe* left his home and was placed in the black iron carriage, his brother-in-law, Reb Yisroel Kazik, had asked him, "Is there anything I can do?"

"Yes, there is," said the Baal HaTanya (the *Alter Rebbe* was called this for the *Tanya* he had written). "Go immediately to Petersburg. Send someone else to Reb Levi Yitzchak of Berdichev, and ask him to pray for me."

At that moment the *rebbe*'s brother-in-law was dressed in very strange clothes. But Reb Yisroel did not protest. He departed immediately, dressed exactly as he was, and traveled to Petersburg.

Meanwhile, another messenger left for Berdichev to inform Reb Levi Yitzchak of the calamity and ask him to pray for the *rebbe*'s release and safety. Being in a rush to leave, the messenger forgot to ask what the *Alter Rebbe*'s mother's name was.

When the messenger told the Berdichever *rav* the news, the *rav* fell to the ground and wailed mournfully. After a while, he recovered somewhat and asked, "How upset was the *rebbe* when this happened? Was he very deeply upset?"

The *chasid* thought for a moment before replying, "Now that I think of it, he didn't seem terribly upset."

"What makes you say that?" asked the *rav*.

"I noticed he forgot to take his slippers, but what was really important—his *tallis* and *tefillin*—he did not forget," was the messenger's reply.

The Berdichever *tzadik* brightened a bit. The *Alter Rebbe* hadn't despaired. All was not lost.

"What is the *rebbe*'s mother's name?" he inquired.

"I left in such a rush, I forgot to ask the name," admitted the *chasid* sheepishly.

The *rav* took a *Chumash* and opened it. It opened to a page in *Parshas Miketz*. The *rav* pointed to the word *shever*.

"That spells *shin-beis-resh*. Shneur *ben* Rivka," declared the *tzadik*. "Rivka is his mother's name." And indeed, that was the case.

Part 2
In Prison

The cell where the *rebbe* was imprisoned was dank, cold, and dark. Into such cells were thrown the worst, most feared criminals, those accused of trying to overthrow the government. The *rebbe*'s enemies had accused him of aiding a hostile country – Turkey. (The truth was that the *rebbe* had done no such thing. The only thing he had done was to send charity to the Jews in Israel, which was then ruled by Turkey.)

The *Alter Rebbe* was anxious to know if anyone had ever been freed from that section. Instead of asking the jail warden directly (for the warden would never answer him), he asked him, "How much do you make a year?"

The warden told him what his yearly salary was.

"Don't you ever get presents from former prisoners?" inquired the *rebbe* innocently.

"Now and then I do," answered the warden.

Hearing this, the *rebbe* felt a little better.

The *rebbe* suffered cruelly in prison. Once he was even placed into a pitch-black cell without any windows. No ray of light ever entered the cell.

The warden wanted to play a joke on the *rebbe*. One afternoon he asked the *rebbe* tauntingly, "Why aren't you sleeping? It's after midnight!"

"Why should I be sleeping? It's two o'clock in the afternoon right now," replied the *rebbe*.

The warden was caught at his own game. "How did you know?" he stammered, flabbergasted.

"The letters of God's name can be made into different combinations," the *rebbe* patiently explained. "At each hour of the day or night, a different combination of these letters shines. That's how I know."

Sometimes important government officials would come to question him. Once an official who had studied the Bible came. "Oh, a scholar!" the official thought excitedly. "Maybe he can answer some questions that have been bothering me. Perhaps you can tell me," he asked the *rebbe*, "why God asked Adam 'Where are you?' Didn't God know where Adam was? And don't give me Rashi's explanation because I know that already."

The *rebbe* responded, "God was asking Adam—as He asks every person in this world—'Where are you in the world?' You have lived so many years already [here the *rebbe* mentioned the exact age of the official, to the official's utter astonishment]. Have you accomplished what you were supposed to accomplish? Have you helped anybody in your life?"

"I accept that explanation," said the official. "You must be a man of God."

From that time on, the official treated the *rebbe* with respect and admiration. "I wish there were something I could do for you, Rabbi," he said one day. "Please tell me if there is anything I can do for you."

"I would like my family to know that I am alive and that with God's help, I hope to leave here a free man."

"How can I let them know that?" wondered the official.

"My brother-in-law Yisroel Kazik is here in Petersburg."

"How will I find him?" inquired the official.

"He will be dressed very strangely. I told him to leave Liozno immediately, and he was dressed strangely then. I am sure he did as I told him to. Just look up and down the streets, and I'm sure you'll find him."

The official rode up and down the streets looking for a Jewish man in unusual clothes. Sure enough, eventually he saw someone like that. He stopped before the odd-looking person and asked, "What's your name?" Reb Yisroel, however, did not give him his own name but a different one. "You're a liar!" the official barked, and he turned around and left, returning to the prison to relate to the *rebbe* what had taken place.

"He probably had someone else's passport and he gave you the name of the person on the passport," the *Alter Rebbe* surmised. (That was indeed exactly what had happened.) "Go again tomorrow," the *Alter Rebbe* said to the official. "Maybe you'll see him again."

Meanwhile Reb Yisroel had discussed with the other *chasidim* this strange occurrence. "It definitely has something to do with the *Alter Rebbe*," they all agreed. "Go out on the streets again tomorrow, and if you see the same official again and he asks you your name, tell him your real name."

The next day the official went out again to look for the strangely dressed *chasid*. After driving in his carriage up and down several streets, he found him. "What's your name?" he asked.

"Yisroel Kazik," came the reply.

The official did not answer. He continued driving down the street very slowly while Reb Yisroel followed on foot. When the official reached his house, he dismounted and disappeared inside.

Reb Yisroel stood on the street, waiting, wondering. Suddenly he saw a note fall from the window. He quickly picked it up and hurried off with it to where the *chasidim* were waiting for him. They opened up the note. "It's written in the handwriting of the *rebbe!*" a *chasid* cried out.

"Look what it says!" exclaimed Reb Yisroel. "*Shma Yisroel*—Hear, O Israel, the Lord is our God, the Lord is One."

"He's alive! Thank God!" The *chasidim* almost wept with relief. "There's hope," they comforted themselves. "Now if we could only find out where he is."

Part 3
Hope

When the *Alter Rebbe* was brought into prison, he was served prison food, which was *traif*. He refused it. Day after day they brought in food, and day after day the food went back to the prison kitchen uneaten.

"He's starving himself because he's afraid he'll be executed," the warden assumed. "Guards!" he called. "The prisoner is trying to starve himself. We must force-feed him."

The guards grabbed the *rebbe* and tried to pry open his mouth and force the *traif* food in. But they could not. The *rebbe* kept his mouth tightly shut. The guards yelled and cursed in frustration. The noise could be heard throughout the prison. The government official who admired the *rebbe* heard it too. He came running to see what the commotion was all about.

"What's going on here?" he demanded.

"The prisoner refuses to eat," the guards told him. "We're trying to force-feed him, but he stubbornly clamps his mouth shut and we can't open it."

"What?" the official was shocked. "You're manhandling

that holy man! What do you think he is? – A common criminal?"

"If we don't force him to eat, he'll starve to death," said the guards.

"I'll talk to him."

The official entered the *rebbe*'s cell and asked him, "Why are you starving yourself? You know it's quite possible you'll be judged innocent and freed. But starving yourself is suicide, and if you commit suicide, you won't have a portion in the next world." (As mentioned before, the official was familiar with Jewish ideas.)

"I am not eating because the food is *traif*. And even if I won't get a portion in the world to come, I will not eat *traif* food," the *rebbe* answered firmly.

"Let me get you some kosher food, then, from a Jewish person," offered the official.

"Right now I am very weak. All I could eat is a little jam," replied the *rebbe*.

"Will you eat it if I get it for you?" asked the official.

"If you yourself get it for me and no one else handles it, I'll eat it," the *rebbe* agreed.

In Petersburg, there lived a Jew who had connections with all the government officers and ministers. His name was Reb Mordechai of Liepli. The official went to this man, whom he knew to be a devout *chasid*.

"I have a favor to ask of you, an urgent one. Can you give me some jam?" the official asked Reb Mordechai.

"Surely," Reb Mordechai replied, taken aback. "But can't you get jam anywhere? Why must it be from me?"

"Because it must be made by a Jewish person," explained the official.

"May I ask for whom it is?"

"No. That I may not tell you," was the official's response.

Reb Mordechai said to himself, "Why would this man want jam made specifically by a Jew? Probably he needs it for a Jewish person who wants only kosher food. I wonder if it's for the *rebbe*." He secretly wrote a little note, which he folded and put underneath the jam. "Who are you and where are you?" he wrote. He signed it "Mordechai of Liepli."

The official brought back the jam to the *rebbe*, who ate it slowly, alone in his cell, and found the note. He wrote back, "I am Shneur Zalman ben Rivka. I am in the Peterpoli fortress in Petersburg." He left a little jam in the jar to cover up the note.

"Would you mind getting me some more jam?" the *rebbe* asked his friend, the official.

"I would be glad to," his friend answered.

He went back to the *chasid* and requested more jam.

Reb Mordechai took the jar from him into the kitchen. There he found the note. His hands trembled with excitement as he read it. It was from the *rebbe*! He was alive! And he was right here in the fortress of Petersburg. Hope sprang up in his breast. He quickly filled up the jar with more jam and gave it to the official. Then he flew off to share the good news with his fellow *chasidim*.

Awed by the *rebbe*'s wisdom and saintliness, the official praised him to the Russian czar.

The czar was curious. "I would like to see this unique prisoner. But I don't want him to know who I am," the czar said.

He disguised himself and appeared at the *rebbe*'s cell dressed in plain clothes. The *rebbe* immediately stood up and bowed his head as it is customary to do for a king.

The visitor protested, "Why do you treat me like a king when anyone can see I am an ordinary person?"

"Because you *are* the king," the *rebbe* replied.

"How do you know?" asked the amazed visitor.

"The kingdom of the earth is similar to the kingdom of heaven," the *rebbe* answered. "When Your Highness walked in, I felt awe such as I had not felt when any of the other officials came."

The czar too went away filled with awe for the holy rabbi.

The officers had a list of accusations and complaints against the *rebbe*, which had been supplied to them by the *rebbe's* opponents. When they wanted to charge the *rebbe* with these accusations, they brought him to a special room in another building.

The officers hurled one question after another at the *rebbe*. "Are you one of the followers of the Baal Shem Tov?" was their first question.

The *Alter Rebbe* replied, "Yes, I am."

The interrogators looked displeased. But the *Alter Rebbe* didn't care. He did not want to be separated from the holy founder of *Chasidus* even for one second.

"Why did you change the text of the *Siddur*?" they demanded.

"Why did you institute the practice of using sharp knives for slaughtering?"

"Why do you tell your followers to spend so much time praying? It takes time away from their Torah studies!"

"Why do you publicly teach *Chasidus*? Doesn't it contain secrets of the Torah that may not be revealed to everyone?"

These and other accusations the officers flung at the *rebbe*.

"What is a Jew?"

"Who is God?"

"What is God's relationship to the Jews and what is their relationship to Him?"

He was bombarded with more and more questions. But the *rebbe* patiently and clearly answered all of them, though inwardly cringing at having to discuss sublime and holy matters with such coarse people.

The officers were very impressed by his clear and logical explanations. Then they charged him with the most serious accusation of all. "Why did you help the enemy country Turkey? That is an act of rebellion against your mother country!"

"I sent charity to Israel, which belongs to Turkey, to help the poor Jews living there," responded the *rebbe* calmly and honestly.

There was no doubt that the *rebbe* was telling the truth. The officers had a discussion among themselves. They decided that the *rebbe* must be innocent. They came to his cell and announced, "You have been declared innocent. You are free to go."

The *rebbe* had been saying the Psalms. He had just recited the verse "He has redeemed my soul in peace." The *rebbe* had been in prison a total of seven and a half weeks.

"Where would you like us to take you?" the officers asked the *rebbe*.

"To the home of Reb Mordechai of Liepli," replied the *rebbe*.

They took him to the house of Reb Mordechai, but instead of taking him upstairs, they brought him downstairs by mistake. In the downstairs apartment there lived one of the fiercest opponents of the *rebbe* who had slandered him to the government. When he saw the *Alter Rebbe* enter his apartment, he almost fainted. But he quickly recovered.

"Please have a seat," he faltered. He brought a cup of tea for his unexpected visitor. But there his good manners ended. His old hatred overwhelmed him. "Now that I have you in my hands, I shall not let you go so easily," he threatened. "I won't let you leave till you sign a paper saying that your new text of the *Siddur* is null and void."

The *Alter Rebbe* prayed silently to *Hashem* to save him from his hate-filled host. "And what gives you the right," shouted the Jew to the *rebbe*, who sat pale and weak after his harsh imprisonment, "to call yourselves *chasidim*? What a lofty name you gave yourselves!"

"Actually, the *chasidim* didn't give themselves that name at all. By heavenly providence it was their opponents, the *misnagidim*, who gave them that name," the *rebbe* answered in a steady voice.

Meanwhile the *chasidim* began to worry. Where was the *rebbe*? They knew he was supposed to be released, but what had happened to him? Reb Mordechai went downstairs, accompanied by another *chasid*, to his neighbor, thinking that perhaps something had gone wrong and that his neighbor would know about it. To their dismay, they overheard Reb Mordechai's neighbor screaming furiously, "And why wasn't *na-aritzcha* good enough for you? You had to go and change it to *keser*? You weren't satisfied with the way our fathers prayed?"

Reb Mordechai immediately understood what had happened. The *rebbe* had mistakenly been brought to his neighbor's apartment. The *chasidim* knocked on the door. When no one answered, they began banging with all their might. At last the door was opened. A shocking sight greeted their eyes. The *rebbe* sat at the table, his head bowed upon his arms, while the *misnagid* stood menacingly above him.

"What's all the racket about?" demanded the *misnagid* as he turned around. He quickly composed his face and lowered his voice. "Here's your *rebbe*. Come and take him."

Reb Mordechai was so angry that he was ready to strike his neighbor. But the *rebbe* motioned to him not to hit the *misnagid*. Shivering with disgust and indignation, Reb Mordechai urged the *rebbe*, "Let's get out of this place!"

"One must give respect to one's host," the *rebbe* demurred gently. He finished his tea and then quietly left.

As they went upstairs, the *rebbe* said to the *chasidim*, "Thank you for saving me. All the days and weeks I spent in prison were nothing in comparison to the three hours of mental anguish I suffered here."

All over Petersburg the news was out: the *Alter Rebbe* was out of jail! *Chasidim* quickly gathered to greet their *rebbe*. How great was their joy to have their *rebbe* back among them once more! After all the worry and anxiety of the past few weeks, their relief and gladness now knew no bounds.

But some *chasidim* were angry. "Those slanderers must be punished," they said. "They wanted to have the *rebbe* executed!"

The *rebbe*, however, would not permit this. He sent a letter to all his *chasidim* warning them, "Do not defame or harm any of the opponents of *Chasidus* in any way. Soften your hearts toward them and love all your Jewish brothers and sisters, even if they are not members of our group. Judge them with merit. Perhaps as a result, their hearts will soften toward us, too."

From that day on, *chasidim* celebrated the nineteenth day of *Kislev* every year, in remembrance of the miraculous release of the *Alter Rebbe* from imprisonment.

REB MENDEL OF RYMANOV

Born: ?

Died: 1815 (5575)

Lived in: Galicia

His *rebbes*: Reb Shmelka of Nikolsburg and Reb Elimelech of Lyzhansk

His successor: His attendant Reb Zvi Hirsh

Best known for: Many great *rebbes* who were his disciples

✳✳ 27 ✳✳

A *Tzadik* Is Born

I am moving away, Moshe," said the *poritz* to Reb Moshe. "Do you want to buy my property?"

"An innkeeper like me does not have much money," answered Reb Moshe.

"You are a good man," the *poritz* told him. "I will sell it to you at a very low price."

The innkeeper went home. "We have a chance to become rich," he told his wife. They gathered up all their money and counted it. It was not enough to buy the *poritz*'s property.

"Let's sell our furniture," suggested his wife. They sold all their furniture. Still they did not have enough money. They borrowed from their friends. Finally they had enough.

Reb Moshe collected the money and set out for the *poritz*. On the way, he passed a broken-down cottage. From inside came the sound of crying – children's crying.

"It sounds like people in trouble," Reb Moshe said to himself.

Seven children sat crying around their mother. "We're hungry! We want something to eat," they wailed.

Reb Moshe's heart melted to see the hungry children.

Said the mother to Reb Moshe, "My husband died. We have no money to buy food or clothes."

What should the innkeeper do? The woman and her children needed help desperately. If he gave her the bundle of money, they would have enough to buy food and clothes for a long time. But then he would never be able to buy the property of the *poritz*. He would lose his chance of getting rich.

Yes! No! Yes! Which way should he decide?

Yes! he decided. He must help this starving family. He must do this great *mitzvah,* even if he might be poorer than he ever was before.

"Here, here is money. Take it. Now you can buy food and clothing for yourself and the children." Reb Moshe pushed the bundle into the woman's hand.

The woman did not believe her eyes. "Do you really mean it?" she asked. The children stopped crying and looked in amazement at Reb Moshe.

"Yes, and may *Hashem* bless you," he said as he left to return home.

Among the heavenly angels there was great joy at this tremendous *mitzvah.* Moshe had given up the chance to be wealthy in order to do the *mitzvah* of *tzedakah.*

"This man deserves a very great reward," they declared.

"But first we have to test him," said one angel. "He must pass the test to receive his reward."

So the angels sent Elijah the Prophet down to test him.

Reb Moshe heard a knock at his door. A strange old man stood there. He said, "I heard about the great act of kindness you did. I would like to have the merit of that *mitzvah* for myself. May I buy it from you? I will give you a lot of money. You will be rich!"

Reb Moshe thought it over. The offer was certainly tempting. It would be nice to have money again. It would be nice to be rich. But what about his *mitzvah*? His precious *mitzvah*? How could he sell his precious *mitzvah*?

"No! I will never sell my *mitzvah*!" he declared.

The old man tried again. "Would you sell me half of the merit of your *mitzvah*? You'll still be rich."

Reb Moshe shook his head. "I will not sell half my share of the *mitzvah* either."

The old man would not give up. "How about one third? How about one tenth? How about one hundredth? Just sell me one tiny part of your *mitzvah*, and I'll make you rich."

"No, no, no, no." Reb Moshe's mind was made up. "I will never sell any part of my *mitzvah*."

Said the old man, "I am Elijah the Prophet. I was sent down to test you to see if you would sell any part of your great *mitzvah*. You passed the test. Now you may choose your reward. You may have long life for yourself and your wife. Or you may have wealth and riches. Or you and your wife may choose to have a child. But," he warned, "if you choose to have a child, you and your wife will be very, very poor."

Reb Moshe and his wife had never had any children. They chose to have a child, and some time later, Reb Moshe's wife gave birth to a baby boy. He was named Mendel.

Mendel grew up to be a great and holy *rebbe*. He lit up the world with his Torah and his many great deeds. Reb Mendel Rymanover was one of the greatest *tzadikim* in his time, born to Reb Moshe and his wife in the merit of their great act of self-sacrifice.

REB YAAKOV YITZCHAK (HURWITZ) OF LUBLIN

Born:	1745 (5505)
Died:	1815 (5575)
Lived in:	Poland
His *rebbes*:	*Magid* of Mezhirech and Reb Elimelech of Lyzhansk
His successors:	Many Polish *rebbes*
Also called:	Seer (*Chozeh*) of Lublin because of his extraordinary vision of people's souls

✳ 28 ✳

The Man Whose Name Shone

On a street in Lublin, a wagon rumbled slowly to a stop. One by one, several *chasidim* climbed eagerly out, excited to have reached their destination at last. In a few moments they would be in the presence of their beloved *rebbe*, Rabbi Yaakov Yitzchak, known to the world as the *Chozeh* (Seer) of Lublin.

"Wait one minute," called the wagon driver to the group of *chasidim*, who were hurrying off. The last of the group, who was closest to the wagon, turned to see what the driver wanted. "I'm not a *chasid*," said the driver, "but I wouldn't mind a blessing from a *tzadik*." He quickly wrote his and his mother's names on a piece of paper.

The *chasid* reached out and took the piece of paper. "Certainly," he assured Yoel, the wagon driver. "I'll make sure the *Chozeh* gets it."

The *chasidim* gave the *Chozeh* their *kvitlach* with the *kvittel* of Yoel among them. As the *Chozeh* opened up Yoel's *kvittel*, he gasped in admiration. "Who is this Yoel whose name shines with light?" he asked.

The *chasidim* exchanged uncomfortable glances with one another. "That's just our wagon driver. He takes us to Lublin every year. He asked us to give you his *kvittel*."

The *rebbe* continued to gaze intently at the signature. "I see from his name that right now his *neshamah* is shining and glowing with joy."

As soon as they were out of the *rebbe*'s earshot, the group of *chasidim* fell into an animated discussion. "We've known our wagon driver for years," protested one. "He's a simple and unlearned person. The last I saw him he was hitching the horses up at the yard at the inn. What in the world could the *rebbe* have meant by saying his *neshamah* is all aglow?"

"Our *rebbe* isn't called the Seer for nothing. If he said it, then it's true," another protested vehemently.

"Why don't we find him and see for ourselves?" suggested a third.

So they all headed for the inn where they had seen Yoel last. They found the wagon and horses there, but no Yoel.

Through the streets and the marketplaces of Lublin they searched, but without any result. Finally, as they headed down yet another street, sounds of laughter and gaiety reached their ears. They followed the sounds till they found themselves standing in front of a house where a wedding was taking place. Inside, people were dancing to the accompaniment of a band of fiddlers and flutists.

Upon entering the house, whom should the *chasidim* see but their wagon driver! He was dancing away, right in the thickest part of the merrymaking. He leapt and twirled with such zest that one would have thought it was his own *simchah* and that his own son or daughter were getting married.

The *chasidim* picked their way through the dancers till they got close enough to Yoel to speak to him. "Who is getting married?" they inquired of Yoel.

"It's the wedding of an orphan boy and an orphan girl," he replied.

"Are they friends of yours?" the *chasidim* pressed him.

"Not really," was Yoel's response.

The *chasidim* would not let him alone. "Well, then, what are you doing here?" they persisted. "And what are you so happy about?"

Yoel saw that his friends would not leave off questioning him. "Well, I see you're very insistent, so I'll tell you the whole story. After you left my wagon to go see the *rebbe*, I went to the inn, fed my horses, and fixed the wagon. I had nothing else to do, so I took a stroll. As I got close to the marketplace, I heard sounds of music. I followed them till I came to this house. I looked inside and saw that people were dancing and singing before the *choson* and *kallah*. The *chasunah* had just begun.

"I stood in a corner and watched the goings-on. Suddenly an argument broke out. The singing and dancing ceased and were replaced by angry shouts and threats. I asked one of the guests what the argument was all about. The *kallah*, it seemed, had promised to give the *choson* a *tallis* as part of her dowry. Unfortunately, however, she was not able to get the money to buy the *tallis*, since she was an orphan and poor. The friends of the *choson* were urging him to break off the match because she had not kept her part of the bargain. They were telling him not to go on with the *chupah*.

"My heart went out to the *kallah*. How devastating it would be for her if the *choson* did not marry her! How humiliating it would be to have the wedding called off! I decided I must do something. I pushed my way through the crowd until I got to the *kallah*. I took out my purse from my pocket and gave her everything I had. 'Now you can buy your *choson* a *tallis*,' I whispered to her.

"After that, the *choson* and *kallah* made up. Everybody was happy again. The festivities got under way once more. As you can see, they're putting up the canopy. The *chupah* will take place any minute now.

"Now, if you don't mind, I'll resume my dancing. It's a *mitzvah*, you know, to gladden the hearts of a *choson* and *kallah*."

In awed silence the *chasidim* left the house. Once outside they broke into amazed exclamations. "What a good deed our simple wagon driver just did!" marveled one of them.

"And he's so poor himself!" another one of the group shook his head incredulously.

"Who knows if that marriage would have taken place if he hadn't done what he did?" wondered a third.

"And what about our *rebbe*?" someone asked. "He saw it all just by looking at Yoel's signature!"

"Well, what did you think? He is the *Chozeh* after all!"

✷✷ 29 ✷✷

The Power of *Teshuvah*

Reb Avrohom Mordechai of Pinczov, a *chasid* of the *Chozeh*, had three daughters to marry off but no means with which to do so.

"You are a *chasid* of the *Chozeh* of Lublin," his wife would tell him. "Why don't you ask him for help?"

Finally he relented and told his problems to the *Chozeh*, who replied, "Go to the town of Krasnik. The solution to your problems is waiting for you there."

The *chasid* took his clothes, books, *tallis*, and *tefillin* and packed them all into a chest. He went to Krasnik and rented a room in an inn there. From the look of the *chasid*'s chest, the innkeeper assumed that his new lodger was wealthy. The innkeeper treated him well, served him hot, cooked meals, and always made sure Reb Mordechai had everything he needed. As for the *chasid*, he spent his days studying Torah, waiting for the *rebbe*'s *brochah* to come true.

Several weeks passed in this fashion. The innkeeper began to get suspicious. "You know," he remarked one day to his wife, "he hasn't paid me anything yet, and he hasn't done any business here since he came. I'm beginning to think he's not so rich after all. Tomorrow I will ask him to pay me. If he doesn't, I'll take whatever he has – though it doesn't amount to what he owes me – and I'll send him off."

That night Reb Mordechai had a visitor. It was the *melamed* – tutor – of the innkeeper's children. He looked very nervous. "I have a confidential matter to discuss with you," the *melamed* said. "Promise me you won't reveal it to anyone."

"I won't breathe a word about it to anybody," the *chasid* promised.

"Ten years ago my boss the innkeeper came back from a very profitable business trip. He had made ten thousand rubles. He put the money into a drawer and locked it up. I was up late that night and noticed that in my boss's excitement, he had left the key to the drawer on the desk. I was suddenly seized by a desire for the money. I opened the drawer and took out the money, hiding it in the backyard. The next day the innkeeper noticed the empty drawer. He became very agitated and began accusing this one and that, but it never occurred to him or his wife that it might be me, because they had always thought I was a very honest man.

"My conscience smote me when I saw how upset they were. I wanted to give them back the money, but I knew my reputation would be ruined then. I was haunted by my deed day and night. Many times I was at the point of returning the money, but I just couldn't bring myself to do it. Everyone would know what I had done, and I would be a ruined man.

"For ten years it's been eating at me, Reb Mordechai. I'm sorry I ever took the money. I have wished a thousand times that I hadn't taken it. I have never touched even a penny of it, although there were times, believe me, that I could have used it.

"Please, can you help me out? Would you give them back the money for me? I can't eat or sleep until it is returned. And don't worry. They'll never suspect you because you weren't here when it happened ten years ago. And I trust you that you won't give away my secret." And the *melamed* handed the ten thousand rubles over to the *chasid*.

The following morning, Reb Mordechai spoke to the innkeeper. "I would like to tell you something private, but you must promise that you will ask me no questions."

"I promise," the innkeeper said.

"Did you ever have anything stolen from you in this house?"

"No, I don't remember anything like that ever happening. Wait. Yes, it did, but it was a long time ago—ten years ago," replied the innkeeper.

The *chasid* took out the bundle of money and put it in the hands of the astonished innkeeper. It was the long-lost bundle with the ten thousand rubles.

"Wha-wha-what's this?" the innkeeper began to ask but recalled his promise and stopped. But perhaps he could ask something else. "Reb Mordechai, what are you doing here?"

"You want to know the truth? I'm not exactly sure myself. I'm only doing what my *rebbe* told me to do." And the *chasid* told the innkeeper his whole story.

The innkeeper realized that he was now in a position to help out the *chasid*. Besides, Reb Mordechai had just done him a tremendous favor. "How much do you need to marry off your daughters?" he asked.

The *chasid* added the figures mentally and told him.

The innkeeper gladly gave the *chasid* as much as he needed.

When Reb Mordechai returned to Lublin, the *Chozeh* explained, "The *melamed* wanted so much to do *teshuvah* that he wasn't letting me sleep at night. That's really why I sent you to Krasnik."

✳ 30 ✳

The Happy Clock

The *rebbe* Reb Dov Ber of Radeshitz, of blessed memory, once arrived in a village as the sun was setting. As there was no inn at the village, the *rebbe* went to the next best place—a bar owned by Jewish people.

"May I have a room for the night?" inquired the *rebbe* of the bartender. "I'll be glad to pay you, but I must have a room where I will not be disturbed."

"I don't really have any rooms for guests," answered the Jewish bartender, "but you can have my room, and I'll sleep in the room next to yours, in the stockroom." He showed the *rebbe* to his room.

Meanwhile the bartender continued to work until the time came for him to close up the bar. He lay down in the bed in the stockroom and tried to go to sleep, but he could not. The noise coming from the room next door was very loud. "What in heaven's name is going on in there?" wondered the landlord. "The rebbe seems to be singing and dancing. What can be the cause of his happiness?"

On and on the *rebbe* danced joyously as he sang a happy tune. The bartender waited, thinking that soon the *rebbe* would get tired and stop. But one hour followed another, and still the *rebbe* did not stop dancing and singing. Finally, toward dawn, the bartender fell asleep. A couple of hours later, he awoke. "I must ask my visitor why he was so happy all last night," he decided.

Before he had a chance to say anything, the *rebbe* approached him and asked, "Can you tell me where that remarkable clock in my room is from?"

The bartender gave a start. "Is it a special clock? I had no idea! But I'll be happy to tell you how I got it." And the bartender told the Radeshitzer *rebbe* the following story.

"A few years ago, a rabbi was passing through the village, when it suddenly began to rain. The rain was so heavy that he could not go on. He asked me if it was all right for him to stay in my house until the rain stopped. I said it was and he came in.

"My guest thought that the downpour would be over in a short time, but it continued throughout that night, the next day, and the following night. During all that time, the rabbi stayed here and waited for the weather to change.

"When the skies finally cleared, the rabbi said to me, 'I'm sorry I have no money with which to pay you, but would you take one of my belongings instead? I have just inherited them from my father, may his memory be blessed.' "

The Radeshitzer *rebbe* murmured to himself, "That had to be the *Chozeh*."

"I looked through his possessions. He had inherited three things: his father's silk *Shabbos* robe, a hat, and a clock. I didn't have much use for either the coat or the hat, so I took the clock and hung it up in my room."

"Was the man's name by any chance Reb Yosef of Tulchin, the son of the *Chozeh* of Lublin?" queried the *rebbe*.

"Why, actually, I think it was!" exclaimed the bartender. "How did you know?"

"Because I know that the clock must have belonged to Reb Yosef's father – the *Chozeh*. The *Chozeh* used that clock to tell when it was time to pray and study."

"But how could you know that?" the bartender asked, amazed.

"Because it's different from other clocks," replied the distinguished visitor. "Usually, when other clocks chime, you feel sad because it means you are an hour closer to death."

"And this clock doesn't make you feel sad?" asked the bartender.

"No. This clock makes you feel happy, because every time it chimes, you know we are one hour closer to *Mashiach*!"

"Now I understand why you danced all night!" the bartender exclaimed. "From now on I will be sure to cherish that clock. I had no idea what a treasure I owned."

REB DOVID OF LELOV

Born: 1746 (5506)
Died: 1814 (5574)
Lived in: Poland
His *rebbes*: Reb Elimelech of Lyzhansk and the *Chozeh* of Lublin
Best known for: His love of all creatures

✻ 31 ✻

The Taste of the Garden of Eden

Reb Dovid of Lelov, of blessed memory, had a very good friend whose name was Reb Dovid of Zelin. Together they would journey to the *Chozeh* (Seer) of Lublin. Sometimes the Lelover *rebbe* would pick up his friend on the way, and then together they would travel to Lublin. At other times, Reb Dovid of Zelin would go to Lelov and pick up his friend, and they would continue on together from there.

Having decided to go see the *Chozeh* one day, Reb Dovid of Lelov went to Zelin to pick up his friend. When Reb Dovid of Zelin saw his friend approaching, he called out excitedly to his wife, "We must prepare a very special meal for an honored guest. From the window I see Reb Dovid of Lelov coming."

His wife was excited to have such a guest. She wanted to prepare a royal feast for the *tzadik*. But in her meager cupboard there wasn't much – just a little flour. For her husband and herself it would have been enough, but for such a distinguished and righteous man as Reb Dovid of Lelov. . . .

She went out into the woods behind the house and gathered twigs. "Now I have fuel for the fire," the *rebbetzin* said to herself as she carried the wood back into the kitchen. She took the flour and mixed it with a little water. She kneaded the dough and formed it into biscuits. Then she baked them. As they baked, a wonderful aroma filled the little house.

Soon the biscuits were ready. The *rebbetzin* arranged them on her nicest tray and served them with steaming, hot tea to the guest.

"These cakes are exceptional!" the Lelover *rebbe* complimented the hostess heartily.

Having eaten, the two friends left for Lublin.

When he returned home from Lublin, the Lelover *rebbe* remarked to his wife, "When I was in Zelin, Dovid's wife made delicious biscuits. They truly had the flavor of *Gan Eden!*"

The Lelover *rebbetzin* could not believe her ears. Her husband had never before seemed to notice what he was served. And now he was praising her friend's baking. How surprising! The biscuits must truly have been remarkable. She had to get the recipe and make some for her husband.

The Lelover *rebbetzin* went to Zelin to pay her friend a visit. After exchanging greetings and how-are-yous, the *rebbetzin* came straight to the point. "You must tell me how you made those biscuits that you served my husband when he was here. I want the recipe."

"Why?" asked her friend, startled.

"Because my husband told me they tasted wonderful, and I had never heard my husband get excited about food before. They really must have been extraordinary. Please give me the recipe."

Her friend gave an embarrassed little laugh. "When my husband told me that your husband was coming, I was very excited. I wanted to prepare something special for him, as it's not often we have a *tzadik* visit our humble home. Besides, he is my husband's good friend. But all I had in the house was a little flour."

"So what did you do?" asked the visitor curiously.

Reb Dovid of Zelin's wife answered somewhat shyly. "I prayed to God and said, 'God, You know if I could I would joyously prepare the most delicious and elaborate meal for such a *tzadik*, with no expense spared. But since all I have is a little flour, God, would You please put some of the taste of *Gan Eden* into my baking in honor of our guest?'"

Her friend chuckled delightedly. "Your prayer was obviously answered. That's exactly how my husband described it. He said it had the flavor of *Gan Eden!*"

❊❊ 32 ❊❊

Napoleon Bonaparte and the Lelover *Rebbe*

Napoleon Bonaparte and his French armies began their invasion of Russia. Napoleon had dreams of conquering the vast Russian army. On the way, he passed through the town of Lelov, where lived the renowned Reb Dovid of Lelov. When the monarch heard about the saintly man and his powers of prophetic vision, he decided to visit him. "Perhaps he can tell me whether or not I shall succeed in my campaign," he thought.

He covered up his royal garments and, disguised as a plain soldier, he entered the humble abode of the Lelover *rebbe*.

"What can I do for you?" asked the *rebbe*.

Napoleon unbuttoned his soldier's uniform and revealed his kingly robe. "I am Napoleon Bonaparte," he declared. "They say that you can see into the future. What is my future? Will I succeed in conquering Russia?"

"What if my answer displeases Your Majesty—will I be punished?" Reb Dovid first had to be reassured.

"You have my word that I shall not punish you, no matter what you say," the king promised.

"Then I don't have good news. You will suffer total defeat," replied the Lelover *rebbe*.

The king's face burned red with rage. Clenching his fist tightly, he hissed, "Rabbi, if you turn out to be wrong, you'll be in deep trouble."

Napoleon and his armies continued on toward the heart of Russia—the capital city of Moscow. They won one victory after another. They captured Moscow. But when they turned back toward France, they found that the Russian winter had set in. The soldiers suffered from lack of food and from the bitter cold. Their morale was low. Now when the Russian soldiers attacked them, Napoleon's troops were too weak and dispirited to fight back.

When Napoleon reached France, he was attacked by the armies of Austria and Prussia. He was defeated and had to run for his life.

The once glorious monarch fled from one city to the next. Soon he neared the town of Lelov. He remembered the *rebbe* and what he had foreseen. "That holy rabbi—he was right after all," Napoleon mused. "I must stop by and pay my respects to him." He found Reb Dovid Lelover's house.

"Rabbi," he admitted, "you were right after all. I would like to leave you my royal velvet mantle to remember me by."

Reb Dovid thanked Napoleon for his gracious gift and the monarch continued his flight. Eventually his enemies caught him, captured him, and sent him into exile.

Reb Dovid kept the cloak. It was a rich, soft, bright red velvet cloak – altogether magnificent. Reb Dovid was not interested in beautiful garments and material possessions. He treasured the mantle because it represented something else to him: the fact that the Gentile nations of the world and their monarchs recognize that the Jews are a godly nation. To him it meant that the following verse had come true: "And all the nations of the world will see that God's name is upon you and they shall fear you."

When Reb Dovid passed away, the mantle was inherited by his son and successor Reb Moshe. Reb Moshe Lelover took the royal mantle with him when he and his *chasidim* moved to *Eretz Yisroel.* There he built a *beis midrash.* For the curtain on the holy ark, Reb Moshe had Napoleon's majestic cloak cut and sewn to fit on the *Aron Kodesh.*

❋❋ 33 ❋❋

Just in Time

Thank you so much for accompanying me this far, my dear brother," said the Lelover *rebbe,* Reb Dovid, to his brother Reb Isaac. "It's not necessary to come with me any farther. You should really go home."

Reb Isaac had planned to walk his brother farther, but he respected his brother's wish. The two brothers said good-bye and embraced each other. Reb Isaac turned and headed back home.

"Why did my brother tell me to go home?" Reb Isaac wondered. "He sounded pretty urgent. I wonder if there is something wrong at home. Maybe, God forbid, an accident happened."

Reb Isaac began to run. Faster and faster he ran. The sweat poured down his face. Panting, he reached his home. "Is everybody all right?" he asked as he burst through the door. "Is Mommy okay? Are the children okay?"

His family looked at him, surprised. "Everybody is just fine," they reassured him.

"Ahhhh," he let out a sigh of relief. "I'm so glad. I was so worried."

Reb Isaac poured himself a little glass of whiskey to quiet his nerves. He picked it up to drink it. Just then the door flew open. A Jew staggered in and collapsed in a faint on the floor.

Alarmed, Reb Isaac rushed over to him. "Wake up! Wake up!" Reb Isaac shook the stranger. Finally the stranger opened up his eyes.

"Here, here, have a little whiskey." Reb Isaac put the glass to the stranger's lips. Gratefully, the visitor drank the whiskey. After a few minutes, he felt a little better.

"What's the matter, Reb Yid?" Reb Isaac asked.

"My wife gave birth to a baby boy last week," the stranger told him. "Today is the eighth day when the baby must have a *bris*. I have looked all over town for a *mohel* and I can't find one. They are all out of town."

"You have come to the right place. I'm a *mohel*. I'll gladly perform the *bris* of your son."

The stranger's joy knew no bounds. "I am so happy we'll be able to have my son's *bris* at the proper time!" he exclaimed.

Reb Isaac accompanied the Jew to his house, where he performed the *bris*. Everybody celebrated joyfully.

On his way home, Reb Isaac murmured to himself, "So that was why my saintly brother urged me to return home right away. Now I understand."

REB CHAIM OF CHERNOWITZ

Born:	1770 (5530)
Died:	?
Lived in:	Bukovina in Carpathia; spent his final years in Israel
His *rebbe*:	Reb Yechiel Michel of Zlotshov
Best known as:	Author of *Be'er Mayim Chaim*

✷✷ 34 ✷✷

The Taste of *Shabbos*

Everyone in Reb Hirsh Masyuver's village in Maramuresh, Hungary, knew Reb Hirsh as "a regular kind of guy." A Torah-observant Jew he was, to be sure, but a *tzadik*? No one would ever have thought of calling him that. Yet what were they to think when one Friday afternoon they noticed Reb Hirsh on his way to and from the *mikvah*? Going there he looked the way he always did, but coming back he looked like a different person. "Look at Hirshel!" the villagers nudged each other. "Doesn't he seem taller than usual?" There was no question about it. Everyone agreed that Reb Hirsh definitely looked taller than he usually did.

"And look at his face!" they murmured to one another incredulously. "There's a light shining there that's never been there before."

All *Shabbos* long, Hirsh's friends looked at him and shook their heads in amazement. Hirsh was a new person—there was no question about it. He looked almost, well, princely.

But when *Shabbos* ended, and the *Havdalah* service was said, Hirsh went back to looking as he always did. Light didn't shine from his face anymore. His height returned to normal. Hirsh was once again an average, hardworking businessman.

That is how he remained till the next *erev Shabbos* when, lo and behold, right before the eyes of his friends and acquaintances, Hirsh became a prince again.

His friends were bursting with curiosity. They had to find out what was going on. One day they surrounded him and demanded, "Hirshel, tell us what this mystery is all about. Why do you look like a changed person every *erev Shabbos*?"

"I got a *brochah*," Hirshel reluctantly confessed.

"A *brochah*? From whom?" Now they were really interested.

"Well, if you must know, from the Be'er Mayim Chaim, the *rebbe* of Chernowitz," Hirsh was forced to admit.

"The Be'er Mayim Chaim! Wow!" Everyone was very impressed because they all had heard about the famous commentary on the *Chumash* written by Reb Chaim of Chernowitz, the *talmid* of the saintly Reb Yechiel Michel of Zlotshov.

"But what were you doing in Chernowitz? That's quite a distance from here," one friend asked inquisitively.

"And why did the Be'er Mayim Chaim give you such a *brochah*?" another friend insisted.

"All right, all right," Hirsh relented. "I'll tell you exactly what happened." So Hirshel told them his story.

While on a business trip, Hirshel arrived in the town of Chernowitz on a Friday. "Where shall I leave my money over *Shabbos*?" he wondered. Then he thought of the rabbi. Surely the rabbi of Chernowitz was a man to be trusted, Hirshel told himself.

He made his way to the home of the Be'er Mayim Chaim and said to him, "I am a stranger here in town and I am looking for a place where I can leave my four hundred gold coins over *Shabbos*. May I leave them here with you?"

"No problem!" replied the Be'er Mayim Chaim.

"And I'll pick them up after *Shabbos*," added the business-man.

They wished each other a *"gut Shabbos"* and Hirshel went off.

A few minutes later there was a knock on the *rebbe*'s door. A woman entered, obviously poor and in distress. "I need help desperately," the woman appealed to the *rebbe*.

"What's the problem?" asked the Be'er Mayim Chaim, his voice full of sympathy.

"My daughter's wedding is scheduled for today. [In those days weddings often took place on Fridays.] But I don't have the dowry that I was supposed to give the *choson*. If I can't come up with it by today, the wedding will be called off. Oh, how humiliated my poor daughter will be! What a disgrace for the whole family!"

Without a moment's hesitation the Be'er Mayim Chaim picked up the satchel of four hundred gold coins that Hirshel had left him for safekeeping and pushed it into the woman's hands. "Here is your daughter's dowry," he said. "Run quickly so you can still have the wedding today."

Astonished at the sudden happy turn of events, the woman sped away on wings of gladness. The *choson*'s family agreed to go on with the wedding, and the marriage took place that day as planned.

After *Havdalah*, Hirshel arrived at the *rebbe*'s home to get his money back.

"I gave your money away to save a young bride from terrible disappointment and embarrassment," the *rebbe* apologized. "Your money enabled this great *mitzvah* to be performed. But don't worry," the great man reassured Hirsh. "In a few days I'll have the money for you. In the meantime may you have great success in your business endeavors."

And indeed, in the next few days, Hirsh realized tremendous profits from his business, far more than he had made before. "This must be because of the *brochah* of the *rebbe*," Hirsh concluded.

The *rebbe* wanted to pay Hirsh back, but Hirsh refused. "I have already been repaid. I made much more money these past few days than I could ever have imagined."

"But the four hundred gold coins are yours. They belong to you," the Be'er Mayim Chaim urged to no avail. Hirsh adamantly refused to take the money.

When the *rebbe* saw that his pleas were in vain, he said, "In that case, I'll give you a *brochah*. What would you like to be blessed with?"

Hirsh could not think of anything. He had everything he needed.

"Since you are careful to keep the *Shabbos* and you entrusted your money to me for the duration of the *Shabbos*, I bless you that for the rest of your life you should experience the true taste of *Shabbos*."

Hirsh returned home to his village. On Wednesday he was already feeling the approach of the *Shabbos*. Anticipation of the holy *Shabbos* queen completely enveloped him. His excitement grew until it knew no bounds. "Do you realize *Shabbos* is coming?" he called out exultantly to his family over and over.

That *Shabbos*, his face was a sight to behold—such radiance! Such beauty! No one could help but notice how different he looked.

When *Shabbos* was over, he became a regular person again. It was business as usual—that is, until the next Wednesday, when the spirit of the approaching *Shabbos* affected and enveloped him once again.

"If you want to see how a plain Jew honors and celebrates

the *Shabbos* the way a big *tzadik* does," the *rebbe* Reb Elimelech of Lyzhansk used to tell his disciples, "go and see Reb Hirsh of Maramuresh. *He* knows how to celebrate the *Shabbos*, thanks to the *brochah* of the Be'er Mayim Chaim, Reb Chaim of Chernowitz."

REB DOV BER OF LUBAVITCH

Born:	1773 (5534)
Died:	1827 (5588)
Lived in:	White Russia
His *rebbe*:	His father, Reb Shneur Zalman of Lyady
His successor:	His son-in-law Reb Menachem Mendel of Lubavitch
Best known for:	His deep expositions of mystical teachings
Also called:	Mitteler *Rebbe*

✳ 35 ✳

Fifty Dollars for *Ata Horaisa*

t was the morning of *erev* Yom Kippur in the town of Lubavitch. In the *beis midrash*, people prepared for the great and awesome day. Some studied *Shulchan Aruch*, others toiled over a page of Talmud, and still others contemplated the spiritual meaning of *teshuvah*.

Shmuel Meir was one of the contemplators. A serious person by nature, he constantly strived to improve his character and his relationship to God. He was known as an *oved*— a spiritual worker.

The *beis midrash* was filled with an intense atmosphere of mounting suspense as the last of the Ten Days of Repentance drew near.

A poor wandering peddler entered the *beis midrash* to rest from his weary travels. He removed his bundle from his back and sat down on the bench with a sigh of relief.

"*Shalom aleichem*, Reb Yid," a Jew offered his hand in greeting. "Where do you come from?"

"Why don't you ask, 'Where don't I come from?' " responded the newcomer. "I'm a traveler of roads. I'm a citizen of all towns. Sometimes I even venture out of the Pale. What doesn't a Jew do to earn an honest piece of bread for himself and his family?"

"And what did you see in all the towns you've been in? How are our fellow Jews doing?" the resident asked him.

"Ahhhh," the peddler let out a deep sigh. "What shall I tell you? To say they are doing well would be a lie. Everywhere the Jews suffer from poverty. Everywhere they flinch at the heavy yoke the nations place on them. Why, just yesterday I passed by the castle of the *poritz* Lubomirsky and heard a shocking story."

"What was it you heard?" asked his questioner.

The peddler replied, "A Jewish family living on Lubomirsky's estate couldn't pay the rent. Last week the *poritz* threw them into a pit. Imagine! A father, a mother, and five children, he threw into a pit! And the worst part is—I shudder to even think of it—if nobody comes to redeem them the count threatened to kill them all tomorrow."

Shmuel Meir had heard every word. He shivered with horror. A Jewish family to be murdered in cold blood? It was unthinkable! "How much did the Jew owe?" Shmuel Meir wanted to know.

"It's a large amount," the peddler shook his head sadly. "Believe me, I would have helped them, but even if I gave every cent I had, it wouldn't come close to what they need."

"Where is this Lubomirsky?" demanded Shmuel Meir.

"Less than four miles from here," the peddler replied. He told Shmuel Meir how to get there.

The *chasid* took off like an arrow. The peddler watched him leave. "I wish him *hatzlochoh*," he murmured.

The frenzied barking of vicious dogs greeted Shmuel Meir as he approached the gates to the castle. "Hounds are not going to stop me from my sacred mission," Shmuel Meir said through gritted teeth. "I came to save a Jewish family, and a few noisy dogs won't deter me."

The count's servants appeared at the gate. They looked Shmuel Meir up and down. Normally they would have chased away any stranger, especially a Jewish one. But something about the way this visitor stood, tall and straight and determined, made them open the gate for him.

"What can we do for you?" they inquired.

"I want to talk to the count," he answered, looking them straight in the eye.

They led him in to see Count Lubomirsky. He sat in a massive room lined with grim portraits of his ancestors. On the walls hung wicked-looking swords and weapons of all types. Enormous heads of hunted deer, bear, and other wild animals stared at him from all sides. Though his heart quailed within him, the *chasid* ignored his surroundings and looked straight at the count.

"What do you want?" asked the *poritz* insolently.

"I heard that a Jewish family was thrown into your pit," the *chasid* bravely replied.

"Oh, yes," the count replied rubbing his hands with glee. "All my friends are coming tomorrow to join me in the celebration. We're going to watch how those creatures are killed."

What barbarity! What coldhearted cruelty! Was this count a man or a beast, wondered Shmuel Meir. But he did not display any emotion. "How much money must I give you to redeem them?" he inquired.

"Those Jews ran up quite a debt. And I'll have to charge you extra because my party will be spoiled," the *poritz* answered. He added it up, arriving at a huge sum of money.

"With God's help I'll get it for you," Shmuel Meir said.

"You have till tonight," the count said grimly.

Shmuel Meir flew from one house to another. There was so

much to do and such a short time to do it in! At each house he told of the plight of the Jewish family. Everyone's heart was touched. No one turned him away empty-handed. Everyone gave him as much as they could, for are not Jews "compassionate people, the sons of compassionate people"?

"How we wish we could give more!" many of them remarked to the *chasid*. But Shmuel Meir thanked each one gratefully because he knew their generosity meant that much less food for their family.

Shmuel Meir looked up at the sky. The sun had passed its zenith. Back in Lubavitch, everyone was probably rushing to the *mikvah* now. Yom Kippur was approaching.

Shmuel Meir was weary, but he refused to dwell on his exhaustion. He concentrated on only one thing—getting the needed money. What he had collected so far wasn't even a quarter of what he needed. At this rate, he would never collect the full amount before sunset. Despair overwhelmed him.

Then a melody suddenly arose in his mind. It was a song that spoke of deep attachment to God. The *chasid* sang the song quietly to himself. A fresh wave of hope washed over him. What greater *mitzvah* was there than ransoming Jewish prisoners and saving them from death? Why, he was privileged to be doing it! All at once his step had a new spring to it.

He looked up and saw the tavern of Solomon Barditsky. Solomon was sitting with his friends on the tavern porch playing cards and drinking whiskey. The fact that it was the afternoon before the holiest day of the year did not seem to bother these heretical Jews. Other Jews were hurrying to make last-minute preparations for the awesome day, but Solomon Barditsky and his cronies simply sat around, their heads bare, jesting and gambling.

But they were Jews after all, were they not? And within

every Jew, Shmuel Meir knew, burns that little spark of God that is called the *pintele Yid*.

Besides, they were rich.

Shmuel Meir addressed them. "I need money to ransom Jewish prisoners. I have to have the money before sundown today. Otherwise, may God protect them! If you do this great *mitzvah* of *pidyon shvuyim*, your reward will be immeasurable. You will have a share in the world to come from just this one deed."

The gamblers stared at him, startled. Would it be yes or no? Life or death? Shmuel Meir waited, praying in his heart.

One man burst into laughter. "I have a good idea," he said. He poured out a tall glass of whiskey before the *chasid*. "If you drink this, we'll give you a third of what you need."

The *chasid* gulped. It was a huge amount of whiskey. Steeling himself, he picked up the glass, made a blessing over it, and drank the fiery liquor. The gamblers counted out the money and handed it to Shmuel Meir. Though his mouth and throat were aflame, Shmuel Meir did not falter. "Men, I need more money. Please save an innocent Jewish family from a cruel death!"

"Fine," they agreed. "We'll give you more, but you have to drink another glass of whiskey."

Shmuel Meir lifted up the glass. "God," he thought, "please give me the strength to carry out this *mitzvah*." He forced down the whiskey. The gamblers counted out another third and gave it to him. His brain reeled. He held onto the table and said, "Just one more third, my friends, and the Jewish family will be free." They poured out another glass. Steeling himself again, he gulped this one down too.

"You're a sport," they cheered him. "Here's the rest of what you need."

His head swimming, his eyes bloodshot, his legs like lead, Shmuel Meir headed back to the count, the money safely in his pocket. He could barely walk. Every limb in his body cried out, "Stop!" How he wished he could rest for a few minutes! But the sun was quickly setting, and he dared not sit down for even one minute.

He arrived before the count. "Here's your money," he said.

"Free those miserable Jews," the count ordered his servants, frustrated that he was being deprived of his entertainment.

Shmuel Meir watched as a rope was lowered into the pit. One by one, the Jewish man and his wife and children climbed out stiffly.

"You're free," the servants informed them.

His task completed, he staggered away.

The sun was about to set. Yom Kippur was almost here. Shmuel Meir had eaten nothing since morning. There was no time to eat before the fast now. There wasn't even time to get dressed. He had to go straight to *shul*. In a daze, Shmuel Meir dragged himself to the *beis midrash*. People stared at him wonderingly. Why was Shmuel Meir sitting in *shul* on the holiest of holy days of the year, on the Sabbath of all Sabbaths, in his work clothes?

Oblivious to their stares, Shmuel Meir felt sleep overpower him. People tried to wake him but could not. "What's with Shmuel Meir?" they asked. "Has he gone crazy?" they wondered. They shook their heads in perplexity.

An hour or two later, Shmuel Meir awoke. An awed hush reigned over the *beis midrash* as everyone prayed fervently, silently. But Shmuel Meir was confused. He didn't know what day it was. Was it Simchas Torah? "Fifty dollars for *ata horaisa*," he joyfully bid, singing the traditional Simchas Torah line.

The congregants gasped. Shmuel Meir had completely gone out of his mind. He could not be allowed to disturb the Yom Kippur prayers. "Throw him out," they protested. The *shammes* approached him, intending to escort Shmuel Meir out.

All of a sudden the *rebbe* Reb Dov Ber of Lubavitch stood up, his eyes blazing. No one moved. No one said a word. They were struck by the *rebbe*'s commanding presence. "Leave Shmuel Meir alone. Don't touch him!" The *shammes* stepped back. "Shmuel Meir is way ahead of us," the *rebbe* explained to the mystified *chasidim*. "Because of his extraordinary self-sacrifice today, he is past Yom Kippur already. His *neshamah* has fullfilled the Yom Kippur service. For him it is now Simchas Torah."

REB SHALOM (ROKEACH) OF BELZ

Born:	1779 (5539)
Died:	1869 (5629)
Lived in:	Galicia
His *rebbe*:	*Chozeh* of Lublin
His successor:	His son Reb Yehoshua
Best known for:	Belz's being one of the largest chasidic groups and still being active today

The Blizzard

nce a villager named Yankel and his son Moshe came to the Belzer *rebbe* of saintly memory, Reb Shalom. "My son is getting married soon," the villager informed the *rebbe*.

The *rebbe* blessed Moshe with the customary blessing for bridegrooms. Then turning to the father, the *rebbe* asked him, "What does a person do when he's in trouble?"

"I don't know," the simpleminded Yankel shrugged.

"He cries out to God to save him," said the *rebbe*. "And if his life is in danger, then he says *vidui* and cries out *Shma Yisroel* with all his might."

"Uh-huh," Yankel nodded.

Yankel did not understand the importance of what the *rebbe* had told him. His son Moshe, who had had some Torah training, realized, however, that the *rebbe* must have a purpose in telling them this.

Father and son set out on their return trip home. The road led through gloomy woods. As they were riding, snow began to fall. They could not see the road. They took a wrong turn and went deeper and deeper into the forest. They had no idea where they were. Soon it was dark. The snow was piling up quickly, and their exhausted horse could not pull them anymore.

"What are we going to do?" Yankel said, panicked. "We'll never get out of here! We're stuck in this blizzard! We could die of the cold!"

"Don't say such things, Father," Moshe gently chided. "Remember what the *rebbe* said to us? If we are in danger, we must say *vidui* and the *Shma* together."

They cried out the *vidui* and the *Shma* with every ounce of their strength. When they finished, they suddenly heard an answering call. Someone out there in the dark, wild forest had heard their cry. A burly man appeared bearing a big stick on his shoulders. Yankel and Moshe watched his approach nervously. After all, he could be a highwayman who robbed and killed travelers. As soon as he spoke, however, their fears melted. "My name is Jan. I heard your cries for help. Let me help you." He took his stick and pried their wagon loose from the snow. "Climb aboard my wagon," he instructed them, "and I'll take you to my house."

The peasant drove them in his wagon, with their own wagon following. Yankel and Moshe went into the house, which was delightfully warm. The peasant was very concerned about them. He gave them whiskey to help warm up their insides, and he fed their horse.

"We cannot thank you enough for rescuing us," the travelers exclaimed.

The man shook his head. "It really wasn't me."

"What do you mean?" asked Moshe and his father, puzzled.

"Well, twenty years ago, I worked as a coach driver for a man," Jan began his story. "However, the wagon and three horses I drove for my master were stolen while in my care. I was scared that the master would be very angry at me, so I ran away. I ran from one place to another until I finally got to a town called Belz. I stayed at an inn owned by a Jewish landlord. He could tell I was troubled about something.

" 'What is bothering you?' he asked me kindly.

"I told him my story.

" 'Why don't you go to the Belzer rabbi? He is very wise. Perhaps he can advise you what to do,' the innkeeper suggested to me.

"I took his advice and went to the rabbi. He told me that the horses and wagon had been found and that I could go back to my master, who wasn't angry anymore. The rabbi told me to promise him one thing: that if a Jew was ever in trouble, I should help him. I promised I would. He gave me a blessing that I would buy a house, a field, and a vineyard. And this blessing has already been fulfilled.

"This night, as I lay sleeping, the rabbi came to me in a dream and said, 'Remember the promise you made me. Out there in the woods are two Jewish people in trouble. Go help them.' But my home was warm and my bed cozy, and outside the night was cold and stormy. So I went back to sleep. Once again the old rabbi came to me and said, 'You must get up right now. Hurry!' This time I got up.

"I went outside. I saw nothing except blinding snow. I didn't know where you were. I had no idea where to go. Then suddenly, I heard your cries. I answered your call. I followed the sound of your voices, and that is how I found you."

Yankel and his son Moshe now understood why the Belzer *rebbe* had instructed them to say the *Shma* and *vidui* aloud. Only now did they realize how much *ahavas Yisroel*–love and concern for every Jew–their *rebbe* had.

REB MEIR OF PREMISHLAN

Born: 1780 (5540)
Died: 1850 (5610)
Lived in: Galicia
His *rebbe*: Reb Mordechai of Krimzitz
Best known as: A miracle worker

✸✸ 37 ✸✸

Reb Meir'l's Revenge

Many people disagreed with the *rebbe* Reb Meir of Premishlan because of his philosophies. The *rebbe* Reb Uri of Strelisk led the opposition to Reb Meir. This is the story of how Reb Meir'l, as he was called, got his revenge against his opponent, Reb Uri.

Reb Uri, who was also known as the Seraph—the fiery angel, had a *chasid* by the name of Shmuel Chaim, who lived in a village near Strelisk. Shmuel Chaim had been doing well in business, but things took a turn for the worse and he lost his money. He was unable to keep up with his debts.

"Why don't you go ask Reb Meir'l for a *brochah*," Shmuel Chaim's wife urged him. "I know many people he has helped."

"I can't do that!" her husband objected. "If Reb Uri hears about it, I'll be in trouble." Their financial situation only got worse. "I guess, I'll go," Shmuel Chaim finally relented.

In Premishlan, he got in line to see the *rebbe*. When it was his turn, he burst out, "*Rebbe*, I'm desperate! Please don't turn me down. Give me a *brochah* that I should make a good living."

Reb Meir lifted his eyebrows in surprise. "A *chasid* of Reb Uri? Well, now I will get my sweet revenge," he said to himself. "Tell me," the *rebbe* said to Shmuel Chaim, "where do you get your flour from?"

"From the village miller," Shmuel Chaim answered. "But I owe him a lot of money. I don't know if he'll give me flour anymore."

"If you tell him that this is absolutely the last time you are buying on credit, will he give it to you?" the *rebbe* persisted.

"Well, I guess so," the *chasid* replied.

The *rebbe* continued, "What about meat? Wine? Fish? Vegetables? Will you be able to get them all one last time on credit?"

"Yes, I think I can," affirmed Shmuel Chaim. "But what will be after that?"

"If you do what I ask, this will be the last time you'll buy on credit. You will prosper, but only if you carry out my request."

"Please tell me what I should do," said the *chasid*.

"I want you to go to your miller, your butcher, and your grocer, and buy plenty of food. Then divide the food in half. One half keep for yourself and the other half tie up in a bundle and deliver to Reb Uri when no one is around."

"I'll do what you tell me, *Rebbe*," Shmuel Chaim promised.

"Remember – nothing – rain, snow, or storm – should stop you from delivering the food to Reb Uri this Thursday."

"I'll remember."

Shmuel Chaim bought all the food as Reb Meir'l had instructed him. He took half the food for himself and put the other half in a bundle for the Seraph. He had no idea why Reb Meir'l had told him to do this. But then how could he have any idea? He was not divinely inspired as Reb Meir'l was. He could not see that all week long the bad weather had prevented anyone from coming to the Seraph and bringing him money or food. Shmuel Chaim had no idea that their home was empty and they had no food for *Shabbos*. In fact, Reb Uri's wife had just asked her husband, "How can I cook for *Shabbos* when there is no food in the house?"

Full of faith in the One Above, the Seraph responded, "Light the oven and get the water ready for the dough and let God provide the rest."

Dutifully, the *rebbetzin* lit the fire in the oven. While waiting for the oven to warm up, she fell asleep sitting on her chair in the kitchen. Suddenly she woke up with a start. Had she heard something? There was no one in sight. Then she saw a large package left near the door. How had it gotten there? She opened the bundle. "Look at this," she called out excitedly. "Fish, meat, wine, flour, more food—everything we need for *Shabbos* and in plenty! Dear husband, come look!"

Reb Uri came and looked. "We cannot use this! We don't know where it came from. Let's see if the *shammes* can find anything out."

The *shammes* went around town asking, looking until he found Shmuel Chaim, who admitted he had done it. "But why?" the *shammes* wanted to know.

"Because Reb Meir'l, the Premishlaner *rebbe*, told me to. He promised me that if I did it, my business would prosper," explained the *chasid*.

The Seraph and his wife were stunned. Reb Meir'l had divined their predicament and arranged that they be taken care of!

The *rebbetzin* turned to her husband. "See how concerned Reb Meir'l is about us! Isn't it time you stopped your campaign against him?"

"You are right, my dear *rebbetzin*," the *rebbe* conceded.

That was the revenge of Reb Meir'l. He paid the Seraph back for his attacks on him by being kind and concerned. As a result, Reb Uri never attacked or criticized Reb Meir'l again.

REB YITZCHAK OF VORKI

Born:	1779 (5539)
Died:	1848 (5606)
Lived in:	Poland
His *rebbes*:	*Chozeh* of Lublin, Reb Simcha Bunim of Pshisscha
His successors:	Many of his disciples, who became *rebbes,* and his two sons
Best known for:	His gentleness and love for his *chasidim*

✳ 38 ✳

The Generous Tutor

eb Yitzchak was a *chasid*, and a *chasid* doesn't ask questions. A *chasid* just does what his *rebbe* tells him to do. So when the *rebbe*, the *Chozeh* of Lublin, told Reb Yitzchak, "Take a job as a *melamed* to teach children," did Reb Yitzchak ask questions? No, he did not. Never mind that Reb Yitzchak was a great and respected scholar, proficient in the Talmud and the Commentaries. Never mind that Reb Yitzchak could have gotten a job as rabbi of a community or been the head of a *yeshivah*. When the *rebbe* speaks, a *chasid* must obey.

So Reb Yitzchak went to look for a job as a tutor. It was not easy. He was turned down one time after another, as he stopped in all the villages between Lublin and his hometown. No one seemed to need a tutor for their children.

Reb Yitzchak did not get discouraged. He went on searching until one day he was hired in a nice Jewish home to teach the children. Reb Yitzchak was successful as their teacher. He was devoted to the children and instructed them patiently and thoroughly. The children and their father liked him very much.

Pesach was approaching, and Reb Yitzchak had to go home to his wife and family. The children were sad to see him leave.

The father said to him, "Here is your salary for teaching my children, and here is a bonus as a token of our gratitude."

On his way home, Reb Yitzchak stopped at a village and stayed overnight in an inn. The Jewish innkeeper and his family were very pleasant and they tended to his needs eagerly, but Reb Yitzchak sensed a sadness in their eyes.

"Why do you look so sad?" Reb Yitzchak inquired of the innkeeper and his wife.

"Please pay no attention to us," they replied. "We do not like to burden our guests with our problems."

But Reb Yitzchak could not bear to see their sorrowful faces. True, they were not his friends or relatives. But they were Jews like himself, and every Jew is responsible for fellow Jews. Reb Yitzchak loved all Jews as if they were his brothers or sisters. And maybe – just maybe – he could even help them. "You must tell me. I cannot rest until I know," Reb Yitzchak doggedly persisted.

Finally, they relented and told him their story. "Our daughter was supposed to get married to a wonderful young man, a studious and God-fearing youth. We had agreed to pay one hundred rubles as a dowry for our daughter. Everything seemed to be just fine. Suddenly, we got a message from the *poritz* from whom we lease our inn. He wanted us to pay one hundred rubles as advance payment for the coming year. If not, he would throw us out and take our inn away. We didn't have a choice. We paid the *poritz* the money. But that was all the money we had. Now we have no money for our daughter's dowry. That is why we are sad."

One hundred rubles. That was how much he had received for his work all winter. And who knew? Perhaps this was why his *rebbe* had sent him to be a *melamed* – in order to help these people.

Unhesitatingly, Reb Yitzchak counted out one hundred rubles. "Please use this for your daughter's dowry," he insisted.

The innkeeper and his family were overcome with joy and gratitude. They could not stop thanking Reb Yitzchak. To them he was an angel sent from heaven. They happily began making plans for their daughter's wedding.

Reb Yitzchak had given all of his money away. Practically penniless, he continued his journey homeward.

Now he was in his hometown. But where should he go? To his wife? He could not bear to see her disappointment when she found out he had brought no money home, especially now that it was close to Pesach. She had probably borrowed money for the holiday expenses, expecting to repay her debts with the money her husband would bring. No, he could not go home empty-handed. "I will go to the *beis midrash* meanwhile," he said to himself.

Reb Yitzchak went to the *beis midrash*. All night he sat and studied the holy Torah there.

Early in the morning, people came to *daven* and study. They saw Reb Yitzchak and asked him, "Why are you here? Why haven't you gone home to your wife? All these months you were gone, and you don't even go to say hello to your family? Reb Yitzchak, what is the matter?"

They pestered him with questions until he finally told them the whole story. Soon everybody in town knew about it— including Reb Yitzchak's wife.

But Reb Yitzchak's wife was not angry at her husband for giving away all his money. She was not disappointed that they would be just as poor as ever. On the contrary, she was proud.

She came running to the *beis midrash*. Reb Yitzchak waited there forlornly. "Reb Yitzchak, I am so glad to see you!" his wife cried, "And I am so proud of what you did! What a *zechus* to have done such a great *mitzvah*! I'm so happy you did it. I don't regret it for one second."

Reb Yitzchak's face lit up with joy. The two went home, and Reb Yitzchak helped with the last-minute preparations for Pesach. They celebrated the most joyous Pesach they had ever had.

The same man who unquestioningly did his *rebbe*'s bidding, who put other people's needs before his own, who gave away all his hard-earned money to help a Jewish family he did not even know, and whose wife was his righteous partner— this same Reb Yitzchak one day became a great leader in Israel, Reb Yitzchak of Vorki, the Vorker *rebbe*.

REB CHAIM (HALBERSTAM) OF SANZ

Born:	1793 (5453)
Died:	1876 (5636)
Lived in:	Galicia
His *rebbe*:	Reb Naftali of Ropshitz
His successors:	His sons, who were *rebbes* in various communities
Best known for:	Being a great Torah scholar and for his great compassion and charitableness

✳✳ 39 ✳✳

Rav Frankel Teomim Takes a Son-in-Law

Part 1

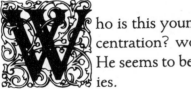ho is this young man studying with such concentration? wondered Rav Yehoshua Heshel. He seems to be unusually dedicated to his studies.

Rav Yehoshua Heshel was a son of the renowned rabbi Baruch Frankel Teomim. He had come to Tarnogrod on business. Having completed his business affairs, he went to the *beis midrash* to spend his spare time studying. Seeing the young man sparked an idea in his mind. "I must find out who he is," he resolved. "Perhaps he will make a good husband for my sister!"

Rav Yehoshua Heshel struck up a conversation with the young student. "What *Gemora* are you learning?" the rabbi inquired of him. The young man told him. Soon the two of them were in a deep discussion of the *Gemora.*

"This young man has a wonderful mind and a deep comprehension of the Torah," concluded Rav Yehoshua Heshel, growing more and more amazed. "And what is your name, young man?" Rav Yehoshua Heshel asked aloud.

"My name is Chaim Halberstam," he replied. "I am the son of Reb Aryeh Leibush, *rav* of Premishlan."

It was time to go. The two of them stood up. The businessman noticed that Chaim was lame in one foot. "Well, no matter," he said to himself. "He is still an exceptional young man, no question about it."

He felt he had to let his father know about him immediately. He got a pen and paper and wrote the following letter:

My respected and beloved father,

I think we have found a *shiduch* for my sister! His name is Chaim Halberstam and he's from a fine rabbinic family. And the way he can learn is unlike any other person his age! I have spoken to him extensively and he is unquestionably a Torah genius. And such *Yiras Shomayim*! He will make the perfect husband for Rochel Feigel!

Your loving son,
Yehoshua Heshel

Rabbi Yehoshua Heshel's letter left out one important fact: the young man's limp.

Part 2

It was divine providence that when the letter arrived, Reb Aryeh Leibush, Chaim's father, was just then sitting and talking with Rav Baruch Frankel Teomin, Rav Yehoshua Heshel's father. He had come to Leipnik to transact some business and had stopped to pay his respects to the great sage.

"Well, well," chuckled Rav Baruch Frankel. "Look what

we have here! A letter from my son suggesting that your son meet my daughter."

His visitor was astonished by the coincidence. "Really? May I see the letter?" he requested.

"By all means," replied Rav Baruch Frankel.

Rabbi Aryeh Leibush read the letter. "This is amazing!" he exclaimed.

"Would you agree to the *shiduch*?" Rav Baruch Frankel asked.

"Of course! It is obviously a *shiduch* made in heaven!" was Rabbi Aryeh Leibush's enthusiastic response.

And so the *shiduch* between the Halberstam and the Frankel Teomim families was struck.

Part 3

Soon the word got out. The rabbi of Leipnik's daughter was engaged. What a *simchah*! Everyone wished each other *mazel tov*. But in the *yeshivah* of Rav Teomim, his students greeted the news skeptically.

"What?" they asked indignantly. "How does our rabbi make a *shiduch* for his daughter with a perfect stranger? We must see him first to make sure he is fit to marry our *rosh yeshivah*'s daughter."

Two students were chosen to go secretly to Tarnogrod to sneak a look at the young Chaim. They returned with appalling news. The *choson* was lame. They did not have the heart to tell this to their *rosh yeshivah*.

Somehow, though, the news reached the *kallah*, Rochel Feigel. She was horrified. A cripple for a *choson*? She came running to her father. "Father, Father, how could you do this to me?" she cried, tears of shame and anger running down her face.

"What is it, my daughter?" asked her father, alarmed.

"How could you make me a *shiduch* with a cripple?" she sobbed.

"What are you talking about?" her father asked in panic.

"Two of your students went to Tarnogrod and saw the *choson*. He's lame! He walks with a limp!"

"Really? How could it be?" He was incredulous. "Your brother never said anything about it! Where is your brother? I want to speak to him immediately. Meanwhile Rochel Feigel, I want you to know one thing. I will not force you to marry him. If after meeting him you don't like him, we will call off the *shiduch*."

Yehoshua Heshel appeared before his father. He could see his father was livid with anger and he guessed why.

"I trusted you, and you deceived me!" Rav Baruch Frankel accused his son. "Why didn't you tell me the young man is handicapped?"

"Well, Father, to tell you the truth, I was afraid you wouldn't consider him if I told you that. He is such an unusually gifted young man that his limp just doesn't matter. Please, Father, have him come to Leipnik and see him for yourself. Once you meet and talk to him you'll forget about his limp right away."

His father agreed, and Chaim was sent for.

Now came a period of waiting. Rav Baruch Frankel waited and wondered if the *choson* was all that his son claimed him to be. The townspeople waited and discussed all the possibilities among themselves. Would their rabbi really consider taking a crippled young man for a son-in-law? The *kallah* Rochel Feigel, waited, too, heavyhearted.

Finally the *choson* arrived. He sensed immediately that some-thing was amiss. He asked questions, and the people admitted that the *kallah* was unhappy about marrying a man with a limp. "Let me speak to her privately," Chaim requested. Chaim and Rochel Feigel met for the first time. He was not a bad-looking young man, Rochel Feigel confessed to herself, but he definitely had a limp. "Please, would you mind looking in the mirror?" Chaim asked her.

She thought, "What a strange request!" but she walked over to the mirror. What she saw in it made her gasp in fright. "Why do I look like that?" she asked, horrified. There in the mirror was her exact likeness, except for one thing . . . she was lame in one foot.

"You were supposed to be born lame," Chaim explained to her gently, "but knowing that I would be your partner in life, I asked heaven that I should be the lame one, instead of you. Now, do you still refuse to marry me?"

His words touched Rochel Feigel's heart. After he said that, how could she object to the *shiduch* anymore? In fact, she thought, she rather liked the young man. She walked out of the room with a smile on her lips.

Part 4

The wedding was carried out with aplomb and ceremony and great joy. Everyone respected and liked the new young *choson*, but none more than the rabbi of Leipnik. "My son-in-law's foot might be crooked, but his brain is very straight," he declared.

In later years, the young man with the limp, Reb Chaim

Halberstam, became none other than the holy Sanzer *rebbe*, of blessed memory, to whom thousands turned for spiritual guidance.

❈ 40 ❈

In the Merit of the *Shabbos*

hatzkel the lumber dealer was a likable, charming fellow. The noblemen in the court of the Austrian kaiser liked Chatzkel and let him have the use of the king's forests to chop down trees for lumber. Chatzkel's business flourished as a result, and he became very wealthy.

Chatzkel enjoyed having dukes and noblemen as his friends. They would frequently drop by at his house during the week. Sometimes they came on *Shabbos* too. They would want to do business with him. "Just sign here," they would say. Chatzkel did not want to upset his nobleman friends, so he would sign. At first Chatzkel was unhappy about desecrating the *Shabbos*, but after a while he got used to it.

Not all of the noblemen liked Chatzkel. There were some who were jealous of the Jewish lumber dealer's prosperity. They whispered false rumors into the ears of the kaiser. "Chatzkel isn't honest. He cheats, Your Highness," they said. "All that money that's going into his pockets really should be going into yours."

One night, while Chatzkel and his family slept peacefully,

police surrounded the house. They forced their way and seized Chatzkel. "You're under arrest," they declared.

"Why?" asked the stunned lumber dealer.

"Our orders are not to speak to the prisoner," replied the policemen.

"There must be some mistake!" Mindy, the wife of Chatzkel, pleaded. "My husband works hard! He's a loyal subject of the kaiser!" The policemen ignored her. Nor did they give any reasons or explanations.

Chained and bound, Chatzkel was shoved into a waiting carriage and driven off into the night. He was taken to a maximum security prison and put behind bars.

His wife and children, however, did not know what had happened to Chatzkel. He had probably been imprisoned. But where? In what part of the country? His grief-stricken wife, Mindy, ran from one friend to another, asking each one, "Do you know where my husband is?" She also appealed to all the noblemen her husband knew. "Do you know what has happened to my husband? Can you help me locate him?" But no one was able to help her. No one knew where the unfortunate man was.

For four months Mindy desperately sought information about her husband, but to no avail.

One day Mindy heard about a *tzadik* with *ruach hakodesh* who lived in Sanz. "Perhaps he will be able to help me," Mindy thought hopefully. She packed her bags and boarded a train for Sanz.

When it was Mindy's turn to speak to the Sanzer *rebbe*, she could not hold back her tears. *"Rebbe,"* she cried, "tell me please where my husband is. He was arrested and taken to prison four months ago, and I have no idea where he is."

"Daughter," the *rebbe* replied in a soothing voice, "ask your husband if he agrees not to desecrate the holy *Shabbos* anymore. If he agrees, he will be released."

"But *Rebbe*," protested Mindy, beginning to cry afresh, "how can I ask him that when I don't know where he is?"

"On your way home, you will find out where your husband is," was the *rebbe*'s answer.

Mindy took the train back home, her mind in a tizzy. Had the *rebbe* really understood her? What had he meant by saying she would find out on her way home where her husband was? And what if – God forbid – her husband wasn't alive anymore? She began to weep softly.

An older gentleman sitting next to her on the train noticed her crying. "What is the matter?" he asked.

Wiping her eyes, Mindy told the gentleman what had happened to her husband. "It's been four months now since he was arrested, and I still don't know where he is," she finished.

"I know where he is," the gentleman said.

"You do?" Mindy's jaw dropped in surprise.

"I am the senior criminal investigator in Vienna. Your husband is in one of my prisons," he informed her.

"Is he okay?" Mindy held her breath.

"Yes, he's fine," the investigator replied.

"Oh, please, can I see him?" implored Mindy.

"Yes. I can arrange that," he replied. "In fact, I'll take you there myself."

Mindy's heart overflowed with happiness. "I hope Chatzkel will agree to what the Sanzer *rebbe* asked," she thought.

The investigator led Mindy to the prison where her husband was. Poor Chatzkel was sitting in his cell looking very dejected.

"A visitor for you," announced the jail warden. He unlocked the cell door and let Mindy in.

"Mindy!" Chatzkel's voice choked with emotion. "How did you find me?"

"It was thanks to the Sanzer *rebbe*. He told me to ask you if you agree never to desecrate the *Shabbos* again."

"Yes, I agree," exclaimed the prisoner wholeheartedly. "I resolve to keep it one hundred percent!"

"I am so happy to hear that. The *rebbe* said that if so you would be freed. Now I'll go back and tell the *rebbe*," said Mindy. She returned to the *rebbe* and informed him, "My husband has resolved never to desecrate the *Shabbos* again."

"By the time you get back you will find your husband home, safe and sound," the *rebbe* assured her.

And so it was. Chatzkel was already home by the time Mindy got there. The judge had found him innocent and released him from jail. Chatzkel went to Sanz to thank the *rebbe* personally for getting him out of jail. Eventually the lumber merchant became one of the Sanzer *rebbe's* most devoted followers. And for the rest of his life, he always guarded the holiness of the *Shabbos* meticulously.

✹✹ 41 ✹✹

If You Can't Pay the Rent, Buy the Village

Shimon was an innkeeper—one of the few positions Jews were allowed to hold. Certainly Shimon was glad to have a job and a roof over his and his family's head, but business had never been very good, and lately it was getting worse. The little money Shimon made went to put food in the bellies of his wife and children and clothes on their back. When rent day came around, there never was enough money left to pay the *poritz*.

Month after month went by without any improvement in the situation. Being a *chasid* of the Lisker *rebbe*, Shimon would now and then hitch up his wagon, visit his *rebbe*, and pour out his woes to him. The *rav* always told him, "Don't worry. Things will get better."

Three years passed. Finally the *poritz* of Skole, who, as far as *pritzim* went, was not a bad man, announced to Shimon, "I insist that you pay me all the rent you owe me for the past three years. You may pay it to me in installments, but I am giving you a deadline." And he named a date in the not-too-distant future by which time the innkeeper had to remit to him the first installment. "If I don't have it by then," warned the *poritz*, "you can say good-bye to the inn and to the village. I never want to see you again."

You can imagine how despondent Shimon felt! Where should he turn? What should he do? "Perhaps the Lisker *rav* will have some advice for me," he told his wife.

The Lisker *rav*, however, could give him no advice, but the *rav* knew that there was someone who could probably help Shimon. That was the Sanzer *rebbe*, Reb Chaim Halberstam.

The Skoler innkeeper had of course heard of the Sanzer *rav*, his unequaled piety, and his talmudic scholarship. It was a good idea, but Sanz, he realized, was a long way from Lisk. "I don't even have enough money to make the trip!" he blurted out to the Lisker *rav*.

The Lisker *rav* suggested someone who might lend Shimon some money. Soon Shimon was on his way.

The innkeeper knew that if there was anyone in the world

who could help him, it was the Sanzer *rebbe*. But what would the Sanzer *rav* tell him, he wondered. He waited impatiently to have his turn with the *rebbe*. With his heart pounding and his hands sticky with sweat, he slowly inched his way forward in the long line.

It was his turn now. Shimon handed the *tzadik* his *kvittel*, explaining his problem. He held his breath while the *rebbe* examined it. The *rebbe* spoke. Eyes, ears, all Shimon's body strained to hear and understand what the *rebbe* was telling him, but what the *rebbe* was telling him made no sense. He was saying that since Shimon could not afford to pay in installments, he should buy the whole village and spare himself the installments.

Since he could not pay in installments – that part Shimon understood. But what was that about buying the village? And the whole village, yet? If he had no money even to pay his rent, how could he possibly afford to buy the whole village?

His mind in a whirl, Shimon said to himself, "The *rebbe* does not understand how business works. This makes no sense at all. One cannot buy a village if one is penniless. Besides, I didn't ask him about buying the village, only about paying the rent I owe."

The people behind Shimon in the line prodded him impatiently. It was their turn now, and why was this innkeeper holding them up? "You got your answer already!" they protested loudly enough so Shimon could hear, but not loudly enough to disturb the holy *rebbe*.

The Jew from Skole had come a long way, and he wasn't going to let himself be pushed about. He planted his feet firmly apart so that he would not lose his place. Perhaps the *rebbe* had not quite grasped the problem. Perhaps he hadn't quite understood what he had written in the *kvittel*. "Rebbe, please! Read my *kvittel* again," urged Shimon, ignoring the impatient people behind him.

To be polite, the *rebbe* picked up the *kvittel* and looked at it a second time. However, much to Shimon's disappointment, he did not withdraw his previous statement.

There was nothing that Shimon could do. With downcast heart and leaden feet, he bid the *rebbe* farewell and headed back for his hometown of Skole.

He was sorry to come home without any good news. He had been to Lisk. He had been to Sanz. He related to his family all that had happened to him. He repeated the Sanzer *tzadik*'s mysterious words. His wife and children pondered his words, but they, too, could not see how they applied to them.

When things quieted down, Shimon's wife told her husband, "The *poritz* sent for you this morning." Shimon's heart beat in fear. His mouth was dry. The *poritz*? It could mean only one thing. The *poritz* wanted to be paid.

There was no use in putting off the interview. Slowly he approached the *poritz*'s mansion. Soon he would be out of a job and a home, with no place to go and no means to care for his family. Only a miracle from God could help him now.

The *poritz*'s servant opened the door. "This way, Master Shimon," said the servant with a bow. Shimon was taken aback. He had never been treated with such respect before. The servant led him to the *poritz*, who seemed pleased to see him. "Please, have a seat," the *poritz* said, gesturing toward an empty chair near him. This was most unusual. Puzzling over it quietly, Shimon waited to hear what the *poritz* had to say. "Do you know what I want to do?" the *poritz* inquired of Shimon.

"I have no idea," answered Shimon, barely daring to breathe.

"Well, let me tell you what I have in mind," the *poritz* declared. "I want to sell you the whole village."

Shimon's head felt light and dizzy. Was he hearing things? So the Sanzer *rebbe* had predicted correctly after all! And he – Shimon – had wrongly assumed that the *rebbe* couldn't understand his dilemma and didn't comprehend how business works. How ashamed he was!

"Since you don't have the money to buy the village," the *poritz* continued, "we'll go to Hungary, where someone I know will lend you ten thousand rubles. The rest you'll pay me back little by little from the profit you get from the village."

Shimon's heart sang with joy. How kind God was! How merciful! And when things had looked bleakest, the most improbable, wonderful thing had happened. *Yeshuas Hashem K'heref Ayin.* God's salvation comes in the blink of an eye. He shook his head incredulously.

Shimon realized the *poritz* was speaking again. He was saying, "And if you are wondering why I want to sell you my village, I'll tell you why. As you know, I have no children to whom I can leave my estate. I have a cousin to whom I was originally planning to leave everything after my death, but something happened to cause me to change my mind. You see, a few days ago, we had some coffee together. Then we played a game of chess. In the middle of the game, my cousin lost his temper. In a wild fury, he struck me so hard that blood gushed forth and I had to be treated by a doctor. I have since decided that he should not be my heir. I would rather sell the estate to you so that my cousin doesn't get it after I'm gone.

And I'll have enough spending money from what you give me from the profits."

So the deal was put together. Shimon owned the village now, and a very rich and powerful man he was too!

Thus the words of the Sanzer *rav* came true. May his merit guard and protect all of Israel!

REB YISROEL OF RIZHIN

Born:	1797 (5558)
Died:	1850 (5622)
Lived in:	The Ukraine, later Sadgora in Galicia
His *rebbe*:	His older brother Reb Avraham
His successors:	Each of his six sons, who became *rebbes*
Best known as:	Great-grandson of the *Magid* of Mezhirech, famous for his princely style and wit

❋ 42 ❋

How to Do *Teshuvah*

A man once came to Reb Yisroel of Rizhin and said, "I sinned and I want to do *teshuvah*."

"So why don't you do it?" asked the *tzadik*.

The man looked up in surprise. "I don't know how to," he answered.

"Well, who taught you how to sin?" the *rebbe* asked him.

"Nobody. I just did it," the man replied.

Said the *rebbe*, "And to do *teshuvah* you suddenly need a teacher? Just do it!"

❋ 43 ❋

The Mixed-up Blessings

Two couples lived in neighboring villages. In the village of A. lived Yossel and Blimi. Husband and wife were a bit different from each other. Yossel, for instance, was a strong believer in *tzadikim*. He believed that with their *tefillos* they could pierce the very heavens and change the heavenly decrees. Blimi, however, did not share her husband's belief.

In the neighboring village of B. lived their friends Chaim Yankel and his wife, Miriam. There, too, the couple differed in their beliefs, only it was the wife who had total faith in *tzadikim*. Miriam was absolutely convinced of a *tzadik's* power to work miracles. Chaim Yankel, on the other hand, was more skeptical.

One day Yossel fell ill. Days went by, but he did not get better. He visited one doctor after another, swallowed one pill after another, but all to no avail. He felt just as sick and miserable and in pain as ever.

"Blimi," said Yossel one day, "I would like to ask a *tzadik* to pray for me that I may get well, but I am too sick to travel. Would you be willing to make the trip for me?"

Though Blimi did not have much confidence in *tzadikim*, she agreed to go. She was, after all, a good wife and knew her going would mean a great deal to her husband. She hated to see him so wretched, and—who knew—maybe there was something to this *tzadik* business after all. She decided to go to the Rizhiner *rebbe*, whose piety and holiness had reached the ears of their village.

Blimi packed her things, hired a wagon, and set out on her journey. As the road led by the village of B., Blimi had the driver stop at the home of her friend Miriam, whom she had not seen in a while. Blimi instantly noticed that her friend was upset. "What is it, Miriam? What's the matter? Please tell me," urged Blimi.

Miriam poured her heart out to her friend. "We are in big trouble. The due date for our rent to the *poritz* is coming up and we don't have the money. We have barely enough money to buy food for ourselves and the children. The *poritz* has threatened to take away the liquor store if we can't pay our rent. He could throw us out of our home, too, if he wants to."

"Listen, Miriam, my husband is very sick. He asked me to travel to the Rizhiner *rebbe* to ask him to *daven* to *Hashem* for his swift recovery. My husband is sure that the *rebbe's tefillos* will cure him. Do you think that a *brochah* from the Rizhiner *rebbe* will help you? You could travel to Rizhin with me."

"What an excellent suggestion!" exclaimed Miriam eagerly. "Wait a few minutes and let me see if I can arrange it." Miriam consulted her husband, who readily agreed. She quickly threw her things into a suitcase. Soon the two friends were on their way.

They arrived in Rizhin without any mishap. However, when it was time to see the *rebbe*, something unexpected took place. Their *kvitlach* accidently got mixed up. Blimi handed in Miriam's *kvittel* and Miriam handed in Blimi's. After the *tzadik* read Blimi's note (which was really Miriam's), he assured her, "The Holy One, Blessed be He, will save you." That was fine with Blimi. That meant God would cure her husband of his illness. She was quite satisfied.

When Miriam handed in her *kvittel* (which was Blimi's), the *rebbe* read it and said that her husband should apply "bankes" – a medical practice of bloodletting that was done in those times.

Bankes seemed a strange solution for someone with financial problems. It seemed strange to Miriam, too, but her faith was so firm that she did not question the *rebbe's* response. If the *rebbe* said bankes, then that's what it had to be.

The two wives returned home. Blimi related the *rebbe's brochah* to her husband, who was delighted and encouraged by it. He began to recover and soon was completely well again. Hashem had saved him, just as the *rebbe* had promised.

Miriam's husband, however, greeted the news suspiciously.

How could bloodletting possibly help him pay the overdue rent? The deadline was drawing nearer. No help was in sight. In desperation Chaim Yankel decided to do what the *rebbe* said. Who knew? Maybe his wife was right. Maybe a *tzadik* did have a special connection to heaven. After all, does it not say, "A *tzadik* decrees and the Holy One, Blessed be He, fulfills the decree?"

And so he bought leeches and bloodsucking worms, which he attached to his body. They bit into his skin and began sucking out his blood. Just then a messenger from the *poritz* arrived with a letter for Chaim Yankel. The letter read, "If the money is not handed over today, your liquor store and your home will be taken away from you, and you and your family will be expelled from the village."

Because no one was answering the door, the messenger let himself into Chaim Yankel's home. How shocked he was to see Chaim Yankel lying on his bed writhing, with blood flowing from wounds all over his body! He did not even try to deliver the letter. Why bother? It looked as if Chaim Yankel were on his deathbed.

The messenger hurried back to the landlord and related what he had seen.

"What are you talking about?" the squire replied heatedly. "I just saw him yesterday and he was fine! Bring him here, bed and all, and I'll see for myself!"

Several servants went to the Jew's home. They bore Chaim Yankel on his bed back to the landlord. The Jew looked frightful. Blood oozed from cuts and wounds and streamed down his body. He was an awful sight to behold.

The landlord's wife recoiled aghast at the sight of their tenant. "What on earth has happened to you?" she cried out, clasping her hands together in dismay.

To his utter amazement, Chaim Yankel realized that everyone thought he was badly hurt. Suddenly an idea struck him. Why not take advantage of their misconception? Here was a way to possibly save himself, his family, and his livelihood—even if it meant telling a lie.

"A terrible thing happened to me yesterday," he sighed weakly. "I rode into town to see if I could borrow the money I owed you. I went to some people I knew, and I scraped together the necessary money. By the time I finished, it was getting dark. No wagon driver wanted to drive me home to my village, so I started out on foot." He let out a long groan for effect and then continued. "It was a very dark night, and there was no one else on the road. All at once, from out of nowhere, robbers jumped on me and grabbed all my money. They beat me up very badly and left me lying there. If not for *Hashem*'s compassion, I wouldn't be alive right now."

"It's all because of us!" lamented the *poritz*'s wife. "It's because he was borrowing money to give us that this happened to him. Don't worry!" she comforted Chaim Yankel. "You don't have to pay us anything. Since you owe money to all those people, we will make things easier for you. For the next three years, you can have the liquor store rent-free."

"Thank you," Chaim Yankel mumbled weakly, sinking back into his pillow, with a hint of a smile on his lips and a song in his heart. What a miracle from heaven! The *rebbe*'s advice, strange though it had sounded, had worked. He must tell his wife that she was right after all. From now on, he too was a strong believer and *chasid*.

The following note must be added: The Rizhiner *rebbe* himself recounted this story to his relative-by-marriage Reb Aharon Karliner, of blessed memory. When he finished the story, he said, "I had no idea that the women mixed up their *kvitlach.* I advised bankes because Miriam's *kvittel* said her husband was sick. Why then did the bankes work for Chaim Yankel? They worked because of Miriam's pure faith, her *emunas chachamim,* because she and her husband believed that the strange advice would work and bring their salvation, and so it did."

REB YECHEZKEL SHRAGA (HALBERSTAM) OF SHINOVA

Born:	1813 (5573)
Died:	1899 (5659)
Lived in:	Galicia
His *rebbes*:	Reb Naftali of Ropshitz; his father, Reb Chaim of Sanz
Known as:	A noted halachic authority

✳ 44 ✳

The Rich *Chasid* and the *Rebbe*

Part 1

In Vienna there lived a very wealthy *chasid* by the name of Reb Kalman Fried. He liked to use his money for good deeds. He provided his sons and sons-in-law with all their needs so that they could study Torah all day. To his beloved Shinover *rav*, who was always helping the poor and needy, he gave large sums of money.

He carefully invested the money of orphans so that when it was time for them to get married he would be able to give it back to them with the money he had earned.

Reb Kalman's main business was growing wheat. He grew high-quality wheat that brought a good price on the market. One year, however, the wheat fields did not produce as fine a wheat as usual. The wheat kernels were small and there were not many of them. Reb Kalman was not able to make very much profit that year. His other investments were also doing poorly. Reb Kalman was getting worried. He must do something. But what? Perhaps his lawyer had some ideas. After all, his lawyer was a clever man.

"Yes, your situation looks very bleak. You are heading straight for the poorhouse!" his lawyer said after hearing the whole story. "But," he continued, his eyes narrowing to mere slits, "you have a way out."

"What is it?" asked the *chasid* hopefully.

"You have insurance on your wheat fields, don't you? If they were to go up in smoke, you could collect your insurance."

The *chasid* jumped up from his chair. "You mean set fire to my fields? And then lie and say it was an accident? What kind of person do you think I am?"

The lawyer shrugged his shoulders. "I'm only trying to help you. After all, you could get ten thousand crowns from the insurance. With that you could build up your business again."

"I could never do that! I'm an honest man!" He stomped out of the room, upset and angry. But when he got home, Reb Kalman heard more bad news. Yet another investment had gone sour. If he didn't do something soon, he would go bankrupt. Then he would have no money to support his children, who studied Torah. He would not be able to help the Shinover *rav* distribute money to the needy. Worst of all, he would not be able to give the orphans back the money that their guardians had had him invest for them.

Night after night Reb Kalman lay awake, thinking. What should he do? He was worried and anxious. He tried not to think about his lawyer's advice, but it kept popping into his head anyway.

One dark night, Reb Kalman went out to his fields. There was a small bulge in his pocket, where his matches were.

The next day Reb Kalman notified the insurance company that a fire had burned up all his wheat. He filed an insurance claim for ten thousand crowns. But things did not go exactly as Reb Kalman had planned. The insurance company sent an investigator to look into the cause of the fire to see if it really was an accident. After an examination of the land, the investigator suspected that the fire was deliberately set. And when he learned that Reb Kalman's businesses were doing badly, he was convinced that Reb Kalman was the one who had done it.

A few days after the insurance investigator had finished his investigation, Reb Kalman received a letter from the High Court of Austria-Hungary. His hands shook so much that he could hardly open the letter. The letter read, "You are accused of setting fire to your wheat fields for the purpose of collecting illegally on your insurance. You must appear in court." The date of his court appearance was a month away.

Reb Kalman thought he would collapse. His heart felt weak. His legs felt like jelly. If the judge found him guilty, he would be sent to prison for many years!

In Europe, a hundred or so years ago, prisoners were thrown into cold, dark dungeons. Most of the time there were no beds or blankets. Prisoners got very little food. Rats and cockroaches ran around the cells. Prisoners were not allowed to have any books or letters, and they sometimes died in prison of sickness or starvation.

"Why did I do it?" Kalman asked himself. "I never should have done it! Now I am in deep trouble! Why did I listen to the evil advice of that lawyer? But it is all my own fault. I knew it was wrong from the very start!"

Reb Kalman repeated this to himself again and again. He felt terribly guilty about what he had done. He could not bring himself to discuss it with anyone. But he needed help and he needed it fast. He had less than a month left.

There was one man who could surely get Reb Kalman out of this terrible mess. Yes, he must go to the *tzadik*, the holy

Shinover *rav*. He would surely be able to help him in his time of distress. But what would he say to the Shinover *rav*? How could he possibly tell the *rebbe* what he had done? The *rebbe* was the most truthful person in the world. He hated anything false or dishonest. "Oh, how could I have committed such a shameful crime," Reb Kalman asked himself over and over. "How could I have fallen so low!" In his heart he asked *Hashem* to forgive him. "I will never do such a dishonest deed again," he promised himself. "I am sorry I ever did it."

And so, filled with thoughts of *teshuvah*, Reb Kalman journeyed to Shinova. At last he was standing before the *rebbe*. But Reb Kalman could not bear to see the *rebbe* disappointed in him. He did not tell the *rebbe* the truth.

"*Rebbe*, he said, "I am in deep trouble. I need your help. I have been falsely accused of burning my wheat fields, and if the court decides I am guilty, I will be sentenced to prison for several years."

"Yes," said the Shinover *rav*, his look penetrating deep into the eyes and heart of Reb Kalman. "If one burns wheat fields, one certainly deserves to be severely punished. After all, it's stealing."

The *chasid*'s tongue went dry. His face burned in shame.

"Aside from that," the *rebbe* continued, "the *neshomas* in the grain were waiting for a Jew to make a *brochah* on them and give them a *tikun*. These *neshomas* will never, ever have that opportunity now."

A choking sound came from Reb Kalman's throat.

"But you said you had nothing to do with the fire. So you have no reason to be afraid. 'Lies have no legs.' The truth will surely come out and you will be found innocent."

Reb Kalman thought he was going to faint. His eyes seemed

not to see. His ears seemed not to hear. He somehow dragged himself out of the room. All hope was gone. The future seemed bleak indeed.

Reb Kalman returned home miserable and depressed. The Shinover *rav* had not helped him at all. He had even seemed to say that reb Kalman deserved what he had gotten. Well, perhaps he had. But would *Hashem* not give him one more chance? He admitted he had sinned. Would *Hashem* not forgive him? In his heart Reb Kalman repented for what he had done. When he *davened,* he begged *Hashem's* forgiveness with all his might and soul.

Part 2

Reb Kalman had a friend in Vienna who was also a Shinover *chasid.* He was the Bikovsker *rav.* Over the years, Reb Kalman had done him many favors. He had given the Bikovsker *rav* large donations of money. Perhaps now the *rav* would help him. Very embarrassed, Reb Kalman told his friend his story. He admitted the whole truth to him.

The Bikovsker *rav* had known Reb Kalman a long time. He knew that Reb Kalman was a good person. It was all the pressure and responsibility for the people who depended on him that had forced Reb Kalman to commit the crime.

"I will go to the Shinover *rav* and speak to him for you. Perhaps he will listen to me," the Bikovsker *rav* offered. "I will go immediately because your court date is very soon."

The Bikovsker *rav* packed up hastily and left for Shinova. On his arrival, he stood in line waiting to see the *rebbe.* When it was his turn, the Bikovsker *rav* said to the Shinover *rebbe,*

"With the *rebbe*'s permission, I would like to discuss the plight of Reb Kalman Fried." The Shinover *rebbe* motioned with his head that the *rav* should proceed. "Reb Kalman is a very kind and generous person. He has helped out many Jews in time of need. I myself am one of those people who have experienced his open hand. He upholds the study of Torah and supports his grown children so they may study. He guards the investments of orphans. He is a wonderful man, full of *maasim tovim*." The Bikovsker *rav* took a deep breath before continuing. "Reb Kalman came to you in terrible distress. He was fervently hoping to get a *brochah* from the *rebbe*. Instead, the *rebbe* gave him a *psak*, a ruling."

"I did not give him a *psak*," replied the Shinover *rebbe*. "I only said that for setting fires, one deserves to be punished. But Reb Kalman said it was a false accusation. So why is he worried?"

The Bikovsker *rav* knew that he was taking a big risk with his next words. After a deep breath, he said, "And if in desperation he set the fire himself, is Reb Kalman totally lost?" The Bikovsker *rav* waited for the answer, barely breathing.

The Shinover *rebbe* answered, "If he himself did it, it would be very bad for him, and if that is the case, I cannot help him."

The Bikovsker *rav* tried one last time. "The holy Baal Shem Tov was different," he said. He knew such a statement would capture the Shinover *rebbe*'s attention. And indeed the *rebbe* sat up more sharply, his clear gaze resting upon the visitor. He waited to hear what the Bikovsker *rav* had to say.

The Bikovsker *rav* began to tell his story. "There was a Jew who worked for a *poritz*. In the mansion of the *poritz* there was an expensive whiskey flagon, standing unnoticed in an out-of-the-way cabinet. Being in dire need of money, the Jew stole the flagon and sold it. The *poritz* soon realized the flagon was missing and he suspected that the Jew had taken it. 'Bring me the flagon or I will kill you and your wife,' he threatened. 'I give you one week!' The unfortunate Jew rushed immediately to the Baal Shem Tov. He told the Baal Shem Tov what happened, but he did not tell him the truth. He said, 'Someone stole a flagon from the *poritz* and the *poritz* has threatened to kill my wife and me if he doesn't get it back.'

"'What do you mean "someone" stole a flagon!' roared the Baal Shem Tov. 'You *yourself* stole it!'

"Dejected, the Jew answered, 'So do my wife and I deserve to die for that?'

"The Baal Shem Tov reflected awhile and then said, 'If you promise me that you will never steal anything again, I will *daven* for you. But remember, you must *never* steal anything again as long as you live!'

"'*Rebbe*,' the Jew sobbed, 'I give you my word. I will never, ever steal again. I promise!'

"'In that case,' the Baal Shem Tov assured him, 'I shall beg *Hashem* for mercy for you.'

"The Baal Shem Tov did indeed pray for him. Miraculously the *poritz* completely forgot about the flagon. He never mentioned it again.

"So you see," the Bikovsker *rav* concluded, "the Baal Shem Tov did forgive that Jew his sin. How then can you, *Rebbe*, not forgive such a dear Jew as Reb Kalman? His only sin was that because of horrible pressures, he set fire to his fields."

The Shinover *rav* sat, lost in thought, for a long time. The story had made a deep impression on him. The Bikovsker *rav* shifted nervously from one foot to the other. Would the Shinover *rebbe* change his mind and give his blessing to Reb Kalman?

Finally, the Shinover *rebbe* broke the silence. "Fine. I will do what the Baal Shem Tov did. Reb Kalman must accept upon himself *never* to do a dishonest thing again, no matter what happens. If he gives me his word, then the Master of the Universe will save him this time and redeem him from his distress."

There was only one week left before the trial. The Bikovsker *rav* hurried back to Vienna, where his friend Reb Kalman anxiously awaited him. The *rav* repeated to his friend what the Shinover *rav* had said.

Filled with joy, Reb Kalman promised sincerely, "I will never do a deceitful act again as long as I live!"

Now that he had the *rebbe's brochah*, Reb Kalman worried no more. He walked around with a calm mind, confident that *Hashem* had pardoned him and would help him.

The day of the trial arrived. Reb Kalman listened intently to the proceedings. The insurance company tried to prove that the fire had been started by the owner of the field. Finally it was time for the judge to give a decision. Reb Kalman was asked to stand up.

The judge banged the gavel on the table. "There is not enough evidence to prove Kalman Fried guilty," declared the judge. "I therefore rule Kalman Fried not guilty. The insurance company must pay him the full ten thousand crowns."

Reb Kalman closed his eyes and gave a long, drawn-out sigh of relief. *"Baruch Hashem!"* he whispered gratefully. "Blessed is the Master of the Universe for this great kindness."

Shortly afterward, Reb Kalman received the insurance payment. He invested the ten thousand crowns into his businesses. Slowly the enterprises began to thrive once more. It took a while, but eventually they were back to what they had been in earlier times. A wealthy man once more, Reb Kalman gave *tzedakah* even more generously than before to those in need. And true to his promise to the Shinover *rav*, he never did anything deceitful or dishonest again.

✳✳ 45 ✳✳

The Girl at the Train Station

The Shinover *rav*, of blessed memory, was standing at a train station when suddenly he heard the sound of someone crying. "Who is crying?" he asked Berel, the tailor, who was also waiting for the train.

"It's a little girl," answered Berel.

"Why is she crying?" the *tzadik* wondered.

"I don't know," said Berel. "I'll go ask her." After a few minutes he came back and said, "The little girl's purse is lost. She has no money to buy a ticket to get home."

The *rav* looked at him strangely. "Perhaps you can help her out, Berel," the *rav* suggested. "One day it might stand you in good stead."

Berel paid for a train ticket for the girl with his money and gave it to her.

"Thank you very much," she said wiping away her tears.

The train roared into the station. Everyone boarded it. Berel stayed on the train until he reached his stop. He got off and went to his tailor shop. A short time later a general came into the shop. "Our soldiers need new uniforms," he told Berel. "We will pay you to make them."

"I will gladly sew the uniforms," agreed Berel. The new job would give Berel a good income.

As soon as the general left, Berel set to work. He bought the material, measured it, and cut it. Then he sewed the pieces together to make uniforms. He made them shorter than the usual uniforms to save money. He hoped the general would not notice.

But the general did notice. When he received the uniforms and saw that they were short, he became very angry. "Soldiers, arrest that tailor!" he ordered.

Berel saw the soldiers coming. Frightened, he sneaked out through the back door, running as fast as his legs could carry him. "The Shinover *rav* will surely help me," thought Berel. "I will go to him." He ran and ran. Finally, he reached the town of Shinova. He entered the place of the *rebbe*. "I am in terrible trouble," Berel cried out. "*Rebbe*, please help me!"

"What is it, my son?" the *rebbe* asked, concerned.

Berel told the *rebbe* his whole story.

"You must go to Vienna and speak to the officer who is in charge of your case."

Berel traveled to Vienna. "Do you know where to find the officer in charge of my case?" he asked one person after another.

"Yes, I know," one man finally said. "I will write down his name and address for you." As he handed Berel the slip of paper with the name and address, he warned him, "The officer is mean. He does not like Jewish people."

Berel was scared, but he knew he must follow the *rebbe*'s instructions. He went to the officer's house and knocked on the door. The door opened. A little girl stood there – the little girl who had cried at the train station. She ran inside excitedly calling, "Father! Father! Come quickly! It's the man who was nice to me when I lost my purse!"

Berel was amazed. "This is a miracle from *Hashem*!" he thought.

The girl's father appeared. "So you are the man who saved my daughter," the officer exclaimed, taking Berel's hand in his. "I have wanted to thank you all this time, but I did not know your name or where you lived. How can I ever thank you?"

"You are the officer in charge of my case," Berel said. "You can help me by pardoning me for making the uniforms short."

"Of course I will pardon you," the officer promised. "I always thought the old uniforms were too long, anyway. The soldiers used to trip on them when they ran. And I will make sure you are paid for the work you did, as well. "

Berel left Vienna with a light heart and pockets full of money. Sitting on the train on the way home, Berel thought about how he had been saved. It was because he had been kind to a little girl. "It is so important to be kind and good to people!" he said to himself.

Suddenly Berel remembered the odd look that the Shinover *rav* had given him at the train station when he told Berel to help the little girl. "The *rebbe* knew from the beginning what was going to happen," thought Berel in wonder. "And then later, when I was running away, he knew just where I should go! What a great *rebbe* I have!"

REB AVROHOM YAAKOV OF SADGORA

Born:	1820 (5580)
Died:	1883 (5643)
Lived in:	Galicia
His *rebbe*:	His father, Reb Yisroel of Rizhin
Best known for:	Continuing the unique approach of Rizhin Chasidism

✳ 46 ✳

Please Do Not Forget Us Either

The Sadgorer *rebbe* was in jail and the Russian government was in no hurry to pursue the investigation. Government officials still smarted from the memory of how the Sadgorer *rebbe*'s father, the Rhiziner *rebbe*, had escaped through their fingers. They would get their revenge now – through his son.

The chief prison warden was an anti-Semite. He didn't mind that the *rebbe* was innocent or that *rebbe* had been cruelly torn from his loving family and his devoted followers. Nor did he care if the *rebbe* suffered physical hardships in prison. On the contrary. He found a special pleasure in inflicting misery upon the *rebbe*.

The warden put the *rebbe* in a dark and tiny prison cell. No windows let in the light of day. There was nothing to sit on. All day long the *rebbe* had to stand. At night a shelf automatically came out from the wall, and that was the prisoner's bed.

Next door to the prison stood a church. At regular intervals the church bells tolled, disturbing the prayers and meditation of the *rebbe*. He would close his ears tight so that the noise would not interfere with his prayers. He had to do this many times each day.

The *rebbe* was forced to share his narrow cell with a room-mate—a vile Ukrainian, Jew-hating hoodlum who ridiculed and insulted the *rebbe* continuously. Coarse-faced, coarse-tongued, and repulsive to look at, he made the *rebbe*'s life miserable. When the Sadgorer *chasidim* bribed the prison guards to allow a sofa to be placed in the cell for the *rebbe* to sit and sleep on, the thug did not let the *rebbe* sit there. Instead, he sat there himself.

At night when the *rebbe* began to study, the Ukrainian criminal would holler in protest, "He's not letting me sleep," until the *rebbe* had to give up and lie down resignedly on his hard shelf.

The chief warden was delighted with the Ukrainian's pranks. The hoodlum had known what to do even without the warden's having to tell him anything. As a reward, the chief warden doubled his food portions.

Seeing that he was rewarded for his mischief, the Ukrainian thought of new ways to torture the *rebbe*. When the *rebbe* *davened*, the thug would sing at the top of his lungs. This made it very difficult for the *rebbe* to concentrate on his prayers. Somehow the Ukrainian knew that this was the cruelest form of torture he could inflict on his fellow prisoner, for the *rebbe* suffered more from this than he did from any physical pain.

One day while the *rebbe* was reciting the morning prayers, the Ukrainian was acting particularly obnoxious, hurling insults, cursing, and singing coarse Ukrainian songs. The *rebbe* could not take it anymore. He could bear physical deprivation, but not this. What meaning did life have if he could not pray to God with devotion? This was the last straw.

The *rebbe* came to the part of the prayers with the following verse.

Look out from Heaven and see
How scorned and disgraced we are by the nations;
Nevertheless we have not forgotten Your name
Please do not forget us either.

Over and over the *rebbe* repeated these verses. Suddenly a change came over the Ukrainian. He became very agitated. He threw himself wildly against the walls of the room, tearing out clumps of hair from his head. At first he could not speak. At last he recovered the power of speech. "Help me!" he shrieked. "He's killing me! Save me!"

His screams echoed down the dark prison halls. The guards came running to see what was the matter. The strangest sight met their eyes. The *rebbe* stood calm and unmoving in one corner of the cell, his face to the wall, wrapped in a *tallis*. Meanwhile the hoodlum was flinging himself in terror and screaming, "Get me out of here! He's killing me! He's tearing me apart, limb from limb!"

A guard ran to the office of the chief warden to ask him what to do. He was shocked to see the chief warden acting much the same as the Ukrainian, writhing on the floor in agony. "Oh, no! Both of them!" thought the guard.

He sped back to the *rebbe*'s cell, unlocked the door, and pushed the Ukrainian with all his might until he got him through the door and out into the hall. As soon as the Ukrainian was out, he stopped screaming and subsided into quiet. Now that the Ukrainian prisoner was out of danger, the guard ran back to see how the chief warden was doing. Lo and behold, he too was coming out of his strange fit.

After that, the Ukrainian adamantly refused to set foot into the *rebbe*'s cell. He was afraid for his life.

The chief warden, realizing he had been punished for afflicting the holy man, humbly begged the Sadgorer *rebbe* for forgiveness. To show that he really meant it, he transferred the *rebbe* to a larger, sunlit cell with a chair and a comfortable bed. He wanted to do more for the *rebbe*. He asked him, "What else can I do for you? As long as I am within the prison rules, I will do anything for you."

The *rebbe* requested two things; first, that his *gabai* be permitted to stay with him, and second that on *Shabbos* and *yom tov* a *minyan* of worshipers come so he could pray with a *minyan*. The warden promptly acceded to his requests.

Eventually the investigation was completed. The *rebbe* was found innocent and released. But the suffering had taken its toll upon him. After having stood on his feet for days and weeks, his feet had grown weak. They never regained their former strength. And from closing his ears so tightly, he suffered the rest of his life from painful earaches.

REB MOSHE OF SHINOVA

Born: ?

Died: 1918 (5679)

Lived in: Galicia

His *rebbe*: His father, Reb Yechezkel Shraga of Shinova

Best known for: Continuing the traditions of his father and grandfather, the Sanzer *rebbe*

✳ 47 ✳

Shmurah-Matzoh Flour for the Rebbe

Reb Avraham Meir, I need a favor from you," Reb Moshe Shinover's letter read. "Pesach is coming and I must have *shmurah-matzoh* flour for *matzohs*. Here in Vienna we cannot get it anywhere because of the war."

"But *Rebbe*," the *chasid* thought when he finished the letter, "it's against the law during wartime to transport food from one country to another. If I am caught, I can get into big trouble!"

It was very risky business to undertake during the First World War, but Avraham Meir was sure that the *rebbe's brochah* would help him succeed.

The *chasid* bought the *shmurah-matzoh* flour for the rabbi and boarded the train to Buda. In Buda he would change trains and go to Pest and from there to Vienna. He placed the bundle of flour on the luggage rack above, next to his *tallis* and *tefillin*.

Cling, clang! Time to inspect the baggage. The transport policeman was approaching his car. The *chasid* trembled. Would he pass inspection? If he didn't, it could mean jail for him.

The policeman pointed his stick at the package with the *tallis* and *tefillin*. "What's this?" he barked.

His heart pounding, the *chasid* replied, "Those are my prayer shawl and phylacteries." He waited for the inspector to ask him what was in the other package, but the policeman didn't notice it. He just went on to the next passenger and began to question him.

"Whew!" Avraham Meir breathed a sigh of relief. The first of the inspections had been passed.

At the busy station in Buda, the train stopped. The *chasid* got off to change trains. He would have to pass the customs officials who inspected all packages.

When an official approached him, Avraham Meir did not stop. Holding on tightly to his packages, the *chasid* just kept walking past the official and the lines of waiting people.

"Stop! Stop!" yelled the customs official. "We didn't inspect your packages."

But Avraham Meir only quickened his step and walked away faster. Soon he disappeared among the thick crowd of people. The official gave up and turned, exasperated, to the next person in line.

The next station was Pest. There the *chasid* changed trains for Vienna. In Vienna he got off. Here he would have to pass customs inspections again.

"Show me your packages," demanded a customs official. Avraham Meir pretended not to hear him. He marched right past the official, clutching his *matzoh* flour tightly to his chest. Avraham Meir melted into the crowd. The official did not try to catch him.

At last he arrived in Vienna. There at the door of the *rebbe*'s house stood the *rebbe*, waiting.

"Praised be *Hashem*!" exclaimed the *rebbe*. "Now I'll have *shmurah-matzoh* for Pesach!"

Told by Yechezkel Shraga Reves,
son of Reb Avraham Meir.

REB YISROEL PERLOW OF STOLIN

Born:	1869 (5629)
Died:	1922 (5682)
Lived in:	Stolin, Russia
Also called:	*Yenuka*, as he became *rebbe* when very young

✳ 48 ✳

Stolin Is Saved

When the evil Balachovitz and his marauders descended upon the town of Stolin, he received a personal invitation from Reb Yisroel Perlow, the Stoliner *rebbe*. "Please do me the honor of having dinner with me," the *rebbe* offered. But Balachovitz had other things in mind. "I did not come to Stolin to have dinner with any rabbi," he haughtily replied. "I am here for other reasons. However, since you were gracious enough to invite me, I will do you one favor. Tell me who your children are and I'll order my men to spare their lives."

Unhesitatingly the *rebbe* responded, "My children? *All* the people of Stolin are my children!"

Balachovitz was taken aback by the *rebbe's* answer. His hard heart softened a bit. "Men," he called out, "we're going to leave this town alone. Let's be on our way."

Thus was the town of Stolin spared from a terrible pogrom.

REB YAAKOV MOSHE OF KOMARNO

Lived:	late nineteenth, early twentieth century (5600s)
Lived in:	Hungary
His *rebbe*:	His father, Reb Eliezer Tzvi of Komarno
Best known for:	Continuing the Komarno tradition of kabbalistic study

✳ 49 ✳

Lazer Is Drafted

Reb Moshe Hersh and his wife, Chana, were heartbroken. First their oldest son, Aryeh, had been drafted into the Austrian army. He had been gone for years, and his parents hadn't even heard from him. But as World War I continued and the Russians advanced, Austria began drafting younger and younger boys into the army. Now Lazer, their seventeen-year-old, was also being drafted and sent to the front.

Moshe Hersh lost no time in going to see his *rebbe*, Reb Yaakov Moshe of Komarno.

Moshe Hersh clasped his hands together pleadingly and cried out, "Rebbe, help me! Lazer was just drafted! Now I have two sons in the army. Do something! Rebbe, please!" he implored.

Moshe Hersh waited nervously for the *rebbe* to respond, but the *rebbe* said nothing. Moshe Hersh waited and fretted.

That *Shabbos* was *Shabbos* Chanukah. The *rebbe* began reciting the Torah portion of *Mikeitz*. Moshe Hersh was called up to the Torah. He stood next to the *rebbe* as the *rebbe* came to the verse, "We could have come back already twice." The *rebbe* suddenly stopped reading, although it was not the usual place to stop. Turning to Moshe Hersh the *rebbe* stated, "Say the blessing after the Torah reading. Your son has been discharged. You can go home now. He is waiting for you there."

Moshe Hersh's face beamed. How happy he was to hear the *rebbe's* words! Lazer had been discharged from the army!

When Moshe Hersh arrived at his home, there was Lazer waiting for him. Father and son embraced. "What happened, Lazer?" asked his father, curious. "Why did the army discharge you?"

"This is what happened," his son explained. "I was standing and watching the wounded soldiers being carried in from the battlefield, and I got very scared. I began trembling. My teeth chattered and my knees knocked each other in fright.

"Somebody saw me and took me to see the army doctor. He burst out in anger when he saw me. 'Are they taking children now into the army?' he sputtered. 'Go home. Here are your discharge papers.' And so I came home."

"Just as the *rebbe* had said," murmured his father in awe. "Our *rebbe* is truly a miracle worker!"

Told by R. Shlomo Akerman,
son of Reb Moshe Hersh.

REB YISROEL ALTER OF GUR

Born:	1895 (5655)
Died:	1977 (5737)
Lived in:	Poland; Israel
His *rebbe*:	His father, Reb Avraham Mordechai of Gur
His successor:	His brother Reb Simcha Bunim
Best known for:	Reestablishing Gur in Israel after the Holocaust
Also called:	Bais Yisroel, after the commentary he wrote

❈❈ 50 ❈❈

Be Strong like a Nutshell

t was Yom Kippur 1973 in Jerusalem, and ten thousand people were crowded into the Gerer *beis midrash*, which normally held two thousand. Everyone was praying fervently, asking God's forgiveness and blessing for a good year.

At three o'clock in the afternoon, the siren went off. The siren meant only one thing – war. It went on and on, wailing insistently, for the tiny country of Israel was once more being attacked by the Arab hordes.

The praying stopped. Everyone was in a panic. What should they do? Should they run to hide in the air-raid shelters? There they would be safe from the enemy's bombs, but to leave the *beis midrash*? To leave the *rebbe*? They could not do that. Most of them decided to stay.

Soon, army trucks pulled up into the courtyard of the *beis midrash* and came to a screeching halt. An officer got out of one and read a list of the names of men who had to go to fight. Hundreds of Gerer *chasidim* were called. These were the men of Jerusalem. Those who lived outside Jerusalem would hear from their local army base.

They had to leave right away, but first they said good-bye to the *rebbe*, the Bais Yisroel. The *rebbe* blessed them. Then they climbed into the convoy trucks, each one wearing his *tallis* and white *kittel*. They might be going off to war, but it was still Yom Kippur. The trucks zoomed off.

With tears in their eyes, their families watched the men go. Would they ever see them again, they worried and wondered.

It was *motzoei* Yom Kippur. The other *chasidim* who had come from all parts of the country to *daven* with the Bais Yisroel on Yom Kippur were anxious to leave. Once home, they would learn if they had been called up by the army and where they would have to report for duty. But no matter how urgent the matter, no one left before bidding farewell to the *rebbe* and getting his blessing.

The line of waiting men stretched from the *beis midrash* outside and snaked all around the block, two rows deep. So many people! Thousands of them, all waiting to receive the *brochah* of Reb Yisroel Alter of Gur.

It was pitch-dark outside because emergency rules were in effect and all the street lights were out. The windows were taped up so no light could be seen from possible enemy planes.

Thousands of people waited in line, yet it was so quiet that one could hear one's heart beating. Everyone was occupied with his own thoughts. Danger awaited them. Would they live through it? The silence was awesome – the silence of the Day of Judgment.

When speaking to the *rebbe*, one customarily wore one's *shtreimel*. But the *shtreimlach* of the *chasidim* were all at home. One of the men, who lived close by, ran home to get his *shtreimel*. He gave it to the first one in line, who, after receiving his *brochah*, passed it to the next one, and so on down the line.

From somewhere – no one knew from where – the *rebbe* had gotten almonds in the shell, hundreds and thousands of them. As each man came up, the Bais Yisroel asked him his name and his father's name and wrote them down. Then he handed the man a nut. "May you have the strength of this nutshell and withstand all difficulties," he said. Each man walked out grasping his almond tightly.

Unlike the 1967 war, which lasted six days, the Yom Kippur war dragged on for almost three weeks. The Jewish people did not see the great miracles that happened in 1967. It was a devastating war. Many Jewish soldiers perished.

All through the war, the Bais Yisroel kept his long list of names in front of him. Whenever he *davened*, whenever he said *tehillim*, the Bais Yisroel gazed at the list and thought who knows what thoughts and uttered who knows what prayers. The only thing the Gerer *chasidim* knew was that there were almost no fatalities among those named on the list. The *rebbe*'s blessings and prayers had borne fruit.

May we merit to have true, lasting peace, with the coming of *Mashiach*.

As told to the author
by Sara Naiman.

REB MENACHEM MENDEL (SCHNEERSON) OF LUBAVITCH, *SHLITA*

Born:	1902 (5662)
Lived in:	Russia; accepted leadership in Brooklyn, New York
His *rebbe*:	Reb Yosef Yitzchak of Lubavitch
Best known as:	Present-day leader of *Chabad*-Lubavitch movement and for pioneering outreach work, scholarship, and prolific writings
Also called:	Lubavitcher *rebbe shlita*

✳ 51 ✳

A Strange Warning

Levi hurriedly opened his telegram. As he read it, his face turned pale – he was being drafted into the army! His wife read it, too, but she didn't panic. "Why don't you go to the Lubavitcher *rebbe*?" she advised. "He will surely give you a *brochah*."

So Levi made an appointment to have an audience with the *rebbe*. While waiting on line, he wondered if he even deserved the *rebbe*'s *brochah*. Soon it was Levi's turn. He explained to the *rebbe* why he needed a *brochah*. The *rebbe* looked thoughtful. "I'll give you a *brochah*, but I want you to remember one thing," he cautioned, gazing deeply with his clear blue eyes into Levi's nervous ones. "Always wash your hands before you eat bread. Don't ever forget that. I wish you success and a safe return from the army."

Levi left puzzled. Why such a strange warning? On the battlefield, one was permitted to eat without washing, according to the *Shulchan Aruch*. "But of course," he thought, "the *rebbe* is very wise, so I will be sure to carry out his advice."

Before he left, Levi said a tearful good-bye to his family, who sent him off with good food and lots of kisses.

Soon Levi found himself in the middle of the war, fighting fiercely on the front lines. He always, of course, remembered to wash *netilas yadayim* before eating bread.

One day, when he was about to start his lunch, he remembered that he had not washed his hands. As there was no water to be found in the army camp, he had to walk down to the river, which took fifteen minutes. He washed his hands in the clear, bubbling water of the river and said the *brochah*.

Suddenly, Levi heard a great explosion. In front of his very eyes, his army camp exploded and went up in flames! The enemy had bombed it!

"Thank You, God, for saving me from death," he whispered, realizing he had escaped such a fate only because he had been fifteen minutes away, washing his hands for *netilas yadayim*. Now he understood the Lubavitcher *rebbe*'s warning. It had saved his life.

❈❈ 52 ❈❈

Chaim Meir Shlomo

How could it be?" the students of the *yeshivah* asked one another. "How could this happen to such a wonderful boy?"

The boy they were talking about was Meir Shlomo. Just a few years earlier, he had arrived in Chicago from Russia knowing virtually nothing about Judaism. But he studied hard and moved up so fast that he was already at his grade level in the *yeshivah*'s high school in Los Angeles.

Then the pain in his shoulder began. Doctors examined and x-rayed it. They consulted with specialists, but the results were not good. Meir Shlomo had a tumor in his shoulder. He went back home to Chicago for more tests and treatment.

How the other boys prayed in the *yeshivah*! How they poured out their hearts in reciting *tehillim* every day! How they *davened* for a miracle for their friend!

Meir Shlomo's operation was scheduled for a Tuesday. In desperation, one of his friends came up with an idea. On Sundays the Lubavitcher *rebbe* met with anyone who came to his door. Perhaps a blessing from a *tzadik* would help, for great help was certainly needed here .

So on the Sunday before his surgery, Meir Shlomo went to Brooklyn to see the Lubavitcher *rebbe*. The *rebbe*'s secretary introduced him, saying, "This is the boy Meir Shlomo, who is ill and needs the *rebbe*'s blessing."

"Chaim Meir," the *rebbe* said. He spoke to the boy in Russian. "May you have good news! May you have healthy news!"

The word spread quickly among Meir Shlomo's friends. The *rebbe* hadn't simply blessed him. He had added a new name—"Chaim"—which means "life." Surely this was a sign of great hope. Perhaps a miracle would indeed happen.

Back in Chicago, the doctors operated on Meir Shlomo, but they were surprised not to find what they had expected. In fact, they could not agree on the nature of the tumor they did find.

The doctors consulted a renowned specialist. The news was good news, healthy news. The tumor was not dangerous. Another operation would be necessary to remove it entirely and to repair Meir Shlomo's shoulder, but he was assured he would be fine afterward.

And, *baruch Hashem*, he is fine today. As I wrote this story, Meir Shlomo still studies in *yeshivah* with the same dedication as in the past. There's only one difference. We don't call him "Meir Shlomo" anymore. He's now known as "Chaim Meir Shlomo."

As told to Rabbi Chaim Zev Citron
by his student Chaim Meir Shlomo
in Yeshiva Ohr Elchonon Chabad, Los Angeles.

※※※※

Glossary

Adon Olam "Master of the Universe." Title of a prayer.

Ahavas Yisroel Love of the Jewish people.

Al Chet Penitential prayer said on Yom Kippur.

Alef First letter of the Hebrew alphabet.

Alef-beis Hebrew alphabet.

Aron Kodesh Ark holding the Torah.

Alter Rebbe First Lubavitcher *rebbe* (literally, "the old *rebbe*").

Amen "So be it." One who hears or receives a blessing says this.

Ata horaisa Prayer said when taking out the Torah on Simchas Torah.

Aveirah Sin.

Baal Shem Tov "Master of the Good Name." Name given to the founder of the chasidic movement.

Baal teshuvah One who returns to traditional religious Judaism.

Baal tefillah One who leads the congregation in prayer.

Bar/bat mitzvah At the age of 13 (12 for a girl), a person becomes obligated to do the *mitzvos*; also the ceremony marking this event.

Batim Leather boxes of *tefillin*.

Becher   Wine cup, usually silver.

Beis midrash   House of learning.

Ben   Son of.

Bentsh   Bless.

Bimah   Platform in the synagogue from which the Torah is read.

Birkas HaMazon   Grace after meals.

Brochah   Blessing.

Bris, bris milah   Circumcision.

Brochah v'hatzlochah   Blessings and success.

Chabad   Chasidic movement begun by Rabbi Shneur Zalman of Lyady, also called Lubavitch.

Chanukah   Festival of lights commemorating the victory over the Greeks and the miracle of the oil.

Chasid (pl. *chasidim*)   One who follows the teachings of *Chasidus* taught by the Baal Shem Tov, who emphasized joy in the service of God.

Chasidus   Teachings of the chasidic leaders.

Chasunah   Wedding.

Chasunah geshenk   Wedding present.

Chazan   Cantor.

Cheder   Elementary religious school.

Chevrah   Group of friends.

Chevrah Kadisha   Society to bury the dead according to Jewish law.

Chometz   Leavened bread or pastry forbidden on Passover.

Choson   Bridegroom.

Chozeh   "Seer." Rabbi Hurwitz of Lublin was called this.

Chumash   Pentateuch, the Five Books of Moses.

Chupah   Wedding canopy.

Daven   Pray.

Din Torah   Civil court case judged by a Jewish court according to Jewish law.

Elul   Month before Rosh Hashanah (August/September) set aside for repentance.

Emunas chachamim   Faith in the sages.

Eretz Yisroel   Land of Israel.

Erev   Day before [*Shabbos* or holidays].

Esrog (**pl.** *esrogim*)   Citron fruit; one of the four species used on Sukkos.

Gabai   Synagogue official; also a *rebbe*'s chief assistant.

Gan Eden   Paradise.

Gaon   Torah giant.

Gemora   Talmud, compilation of the Oral Torah.

Gut yontif   "Happy Holiday." Greeting given on the festival.

Hachnosas orchim   Hospitality.

Haggadah   Story of Passover recited at the *seder*.

Hakofos   Circling the *bimah* while dancing with the Torah on Simchas Torah.

Halachah (**adj. halachic**)   Jewish law.

Hallel   Prayer of praise said on joyous occasions.

Hashem   God.

Hatzlochoh   Success.

Havdalah   Prayer marking the end of *Shabbos*.

Kaddish   Public prayer of praise to God; also prayer said by mourners.

Kallah   Bride.

Kavanah   Feeling (as in praying with feeling).

Keser   Crown.

Kfitzas haderech   "Jumping of the way." Phenomenon of covering a great distance in a short span of time.

Kichel   Biscuit.

Kiddush   Blessing said over the wine on *Shabbos* and festivals.

Kislev   Fourth month of the year. Chanukah falls in this month.

Kittel   White robe worn on Yom Kippur.

Kol Nidrei   Solemn prayer recited Yom Kippur eve.

Kvittel (**pl.** *kvitlach*)   Note asking for a blessing that a *chasid* gives to his *rebbe*.

L'chaim   "To life."

Lekovod Shabbos   In honor of the *Shabbos*.

Levayah   Funeral.

Lulav   Palm branch used on the holiday of Sukkos.

Maariv   Evening prayer.

Maasim tovim   Good deeds.

Machnis orach   Host.

Magid   Preacher of Torah.

Malach   Angel.

Mashiach   Messiah. One of the foundations of Judaism is to believe in the coming of *Mashiach*.

Matzoh   Unleavened bread eaten on Pesach.

Mazel tov   "Congratulations." Said upon the birth of child or at weddings, *bar mitzvah*s, or happy occasions.

Megillah   Scroll, especially the Book of Esther, which is read on Purim.

Melamed   Teacher.

Mesader kidushin   One who performs a marriage ceremony.

Mikvah   Ritual bath.

Minchah   Afternoon prayer.

Minyan   Required number of ten for public prayer.

Mishnah   First compilation of the Oral Law.

Misnagid (**pl.** *misnagdim*)   Opponent of Chasidism.

Mitzvah (**pl.** *mitzvos*)   Torah commandment.

Motzoei **Yom Kippur**   Evening or day after Yom Kippur.

Na-artizcha   First word of a public prayer.

Negel vasser   Ritual hand washing done upon arising.

Neila   Last prayer said on Yom Kippur. Literally, the closing of the gate.

Neshamah (**pl.** *neshomas*)   Soul.

Netilas yadayim   Ritual washing of the hands done before eating bread.

Nigun   Melody.

Olam habo   World to come.

Oved   One who serves God.

Parnosoh   A living.

Parshas Miketz   Torah portion called *Miketz*.

Parshios   Torah portions read every week in the synagogue.

Payos   Hair on the temples, which the Torah requires men to grow.

Pesach   Holiday of Passover commemorating the redemption of the Jews out of slavery in Egypt.

Pidyon shvuyim   Ransoming prisoners.

Pintele Yid   "Jewish spark."

Poritz (**pl.** *Pritzim*)   Squire, landowner. Often the *poritz* owned the whole village.

Psak   Jewish legal ruling.

Purim   Festival commemorating the deliverance of the Jews from destruction by Haman.

Rav   Rabbi.

Reb   Title of respect.

Rebbe   Chasidic leader.

Rebbetzin   Rabbi's wife.

Rosh Hashanah   Jewish new year.

Ruach hakodesh   Prophetic vision.

Rosh yeshivah   Head of a *yeshivah*.

Samovar   Teakettle.

Seder   Ceremony of recounting the Passover story and eating the *matzoh,* usually done with family and friends.

Sefer **(pl. *seforim*)**   Book on a Torah topic.

Sefer Torah   Torah scroll.

Seudah   Meal.

Shabbos   Sabbath day of rest and spiritual rejuvenation.

Shachris   Morning prayer.

Shalach monos   Gifts sent and exchanged on Purim.

Shalom, shalom aleichem   "Peace, Peace to you." Traditional greeting.

Shalosh seudos   Third meal eaten *Shabbos* afternoon.

Shammes   Sexton, caretaker of synagogue, assistant to rabbi.

Shatnes   Forbidden garment of wool and linen.

Shechinah   God's presence.

Sheva Brochos   "Seven blessings." Prayers said at a wedding and at celebrations for seven days after the wedding.

Shiduch   Marriage match.

Shlita   "May he live many long and good years."

Shma Yisroel   "Hear, O Israel" (a prayer).

Shtetl   Village.

Shtreimel **(pl. *shtreimlach*)**   Fur hat worn on Sabbath and festivals by many *chasidim.*

Shul   Synagogue.

Shulchan Aruch   Code of Jewish law.

Simchah   Joyous occasion.

Simchas Torah   Joyous festival that marks the completion of the annual cycle of Torah reading in the synagogue.

Siyum   Completion of a talmudic tractate; celebration at that completion.

Sukkah (**pl.** *sukkos*) "Booth" structure without a roof covered with foliage in which Jews live during the festival of Sukkos.

Sukkos Festival commemorating the Jewish people's living in "booths" after the Exodus from Egypt.

Tallis Prayer shawl.

Tallis koton Fringed garment usually worn under the shirt.

Talmid (**pl.** *talmidim*) Student.

Tanya Book of chasidic teachings by Rabbi Shneur Zalman of Lyady.

Techum Shabbos Distance one is allowed to walk on *Shabbos* outside the city (about 1 kilometer).

Tefillah (**pl.** *tefilos*) Prayer.

Tefillin Leather boxes containing passages of the Torah and worn every weekday morning during prayers.

Tehillim Psalms.

Teshuvah Repentance.

Tikun Literally, "fixing." Advice as to how to rectify a sin or error a person committed.

Tikun Chatzos Prayer said at midnight to mourn the destruction of the Temple.

Tochter Daughter (Yiddish).

Traif Not kosher; forbidden to eat.

Tuf Last letter of the Hebrew alphabet.

Tzadik (**pl.** *tzadikim*) Righteous person.

Tzedakah Charity (literally, "act of righteousness").

Ushpizin Seven spiritual guests on Sukkos—the patriarchs, etc.

Vidui Confessional prayer said on Yom Kippur and right before death.

Yahrzeit Anniversary of a death.

Yeshivah Academy of talmudic learning.

Yeshuos Yaakov Title of scholarly work by Rabbi Yaakov Orenstein.

Yiras Shomayim Awe of God.

Yom Kippur Day of Atonement on which Jews fast and pray in the synagogue.

Yoma Tractate in the Talmud.

Yom tov Holiday.

Zechus Merit.

Zeide Grandfather.

References

Alter, Avrohom Mordechai. *B'Darkei Polin Ho'Avelos*. Jerusalem: Machon Zecher Naftoli, 1987.

Amudei Chesed (pamphlet, n.d.).

Bakhon, Chaim Dovid. *Der Shinover Rav*. Brooklyn, NY: Mosad Zecher Naftoli, 1987.

Bickmeister, Rabbi Yisroel. *Sipurei Niflaos Migdolei Yisroel*. 1969.

De Chozeh (pamphlet, n.d.).

Derech Tzadikim. Jerusalem: Pinchos Dovid Veberman, n.d.

Emunas Yisroel (pamphlet, n.d.).

Gafner, Yaakov Shalom. *Or HaGalil*. Jerusalem: Baruch B. Friedman, n.d.

Glitzenstein, Rav Avraham Chanoch. *Sefer HaToldos – Rabi Shneur Zalman Rabeinu HaZaken*. Brooklyn, NY: Kehot Publishing Company, 1986.

Gottlieb, N. T. *Amudei Torah*. Jerusalem: Machon Gacheles, 1989.

Kadaner, Rav Yaakov. *Niflaos HaTzadikim*. Lemberg: Avraham Nissan Zis, n.d.

———. *Sipurim Noraim*. Lemberg: Avraham Nissan Zis, n.d.

Mordechai ben Yechhezel. *Sefer HaMaasiyos*. Tel Aviv: Dvir Company, 1965.

Niflaos Yisroel (pamphlet, n.d.).

Raphael, Yitzchok. *Sefer HaChasidus*. Tel Aviv: A. Zioni Publishing House, 1961.

Sipurim Noraim B'Yiddish. Brooklyn, NY: Bais Hillel, 1987.

Weinfeld, S. *Maasei HaTzadikim*. Jerusalem, 1959.

Weinstock, Rabbi Moshe Yair. *Kodesh Hillulim*. Brooklyn, NY, 1978.

Zevin, HaRav Shlomo Yosef. *Sipurei Chasidim*. Jerusalem: Bais Hillel, n.d.

❉❉❉❉❉

About the Author

Sterna Citron comes from distinguished families on both her paternal and maternal sides. Her late father, Rabbi Eli Chaim Carlebach, was a scholar, writer, and publisher. The Carlebach family was one of the most outstanding rabbinic families of Germany. Her maternal grandfather, Rabbi Shneur Zalman Schneerson, was descended from the founder of *Chabad* Chasidism, the Baal HaTanya, and from Reb Levi Yitzchak of Berdichev. He was a cousin of the present Lubavitcher *rebbe,* Rabbi Menachem Mendel Schneerson.

Mrs. Citron is a teacher at Bais Yaakov High School for Girls in Los Angeles, California, as well as the editor of *The Jewish Reader,* a magazine for children. Previously she was one of the editors of *A Student's Obligation: Advice from the Rebbe of the Warsaw Ghetto* by Kalonymus Kalman Shapira and of *Light of Life,* a compendium of the writings of Rabbi Chaim ben Attar.

Mrs. Citron lives with her husband and four children in Los Angeles.